Leadership

Stop Being Stupid And Take The Road Less Traveled To

Greatly Achieve Full Control Of Your Life By Rising Trust,

Influence, Strong Relationships And Daring Communication

For Management

Mel Blenchard

- CHAPTER 1: PREPARING YOURSELF FOR LEADERSHIP 1
- CHAPTER 2: HABITS OF HIGHLY EFFECTIVE LEADERS 8
- CHAPTER 3: DEALING WITH SELF-DOUBT 19
- CHAPTER 4: HIERARCHY OF LEADERSHIP 27
- CHAPTER 5: GOING THROUGH LEADERSHIP CHALLENGES 32
- CHAPTER 6: THE TRAITS OF A GOOD LEADER, AND HOW TO DEVELOP THEM 36
- CHAPTER 7: COMMUNICATION AND HUMILITY 44
- CHAPTER 8: ALWAYS THINK ABOUT NUMBER #1 50
- CHAPTER 9: HOW TO ADD VALUE TO OTHER PEOPLE'S LIFE 60
- CHAPTER 10: PRACTICING LEADERSHIP 69
- CHAPTER 11: THE HONEST LEADER 79
- CHAPTER 12: COMMUNICATING LIKE A TRUE LEADER 83
- CHAPTER 13: ON LEADERSHIP QUALITIES 87
- CHAPTER 14: LEADERSHIP EXAMPLES AND SCENARIOS ... 93
- CHAPTER 15: HOW TO INFLUENCE PEOPLE? 104
- CHAPTER 16: DON'T BE LED – BREAKING THE INVISIBLE LEAD 110
- CHAPTER 17: COMMUNICATION AND MANAGEMENT SKILLS 113
- CHAPTER 18: 7 STEPS TO GROWING A SUCCESSFUL TEAM 119

CHAPTER 19: 10 TIPS TO BECOME A MORE EFFECTIVE LEADER 124

CHAPTER 20: THE IMPORTANCE OF LEADERSHIP IN BUSINESS 130

CHAPTER 21: LEARN TO BE TRUSTWORTHY 146

CHAPTER 22: COMMITMENT 149

CHAPTER 23: BODY LANGUAGE IS KEY TO LEADERSHIP . 153

CHAPTER 24: BE A POSITIVE INFLUENCE TO OTHERS 158

CHAPTER 25: THE HIGH-YIELDING DIVIDEND STOCKS 168

CHAPTER 26: WORK–LIFE INTEGRATION—BALANCE IS SO PASSÉ! 174

CHAPTER 27: SUBTLE TRICKS TO INFLUENCE PEOPLE 186

CHAPTER 28: MAKE SURE TO STIMULATE THE INTELLECT 197

CHAPTER 29: HOW TO IMPROVE YOUR MANAGEMENT SKILLS 202

CHAPTER 30: MANAGEMENT PRINCIPLES TO FOLLOW WHEN DEALING WITH DIFFICULT PEOPLE 209

CHAPTER 31: FOCUS ON RESULTS 215

CHAPTER 32: SOCIAL DYNAMICS 219

CHAPTER 33: LEADERSHIP DIRECTION 223

CHAPTER 34: KNOW HOW TO HARNESS THE BENEFITS OF CONNECTIONS 230

CHAPTER 35: DELEGATE AND GET THINGS DONE 235

Chapter 1: Preparing Yourself For Leadership

As an adult, you are guiding the other members of your family; if you are a parent, you are leading your children. In high school, you probably led your classmates through a class project, or maybe you have led a small group of your college mates when you have organized the annual debate competition.

You have probably driven your friends through a hiking expedition, or your parents through a holiday cruise. Even at work, you have become a leader momentarily when you have discussed a new project in a meeting, or when you have led the other members in your department to work on your dream project.

My point is: we have all, knowingly or unknowingly, acted as a leader in some situations of our lives, albeit in a small way. We have all been a leader - and a great one at that - at some point, and if we have done it once, we can surely do it again.

You don't need to be in charge of a large team - who will do your bidding; no questions asked - to be considered a leader, although that could be your goal at the end. You don't need a group of people cheering and following you're every word to know that you are a successful leader. You will know so yourself when you can see that you have succeeded in motivation even a smaller group of people to respect and admire you.

Preparing Yourself

A good leader is a mix of a handful of good qualities - honesty, dedication, commitment, confidence and decisiveness - and something more. This concept of 'something more' is what will set you apart from everyone else, and we will now learn of some ways that you can prepare yourself to be a leader.

● Analyze yourself, honestly

Before we start on this journey, the first step for you to examine yourself, in the most honest way possible. List all your gifts and faults so that you can truly see the person that you are. Ask yourself:

○ Am I an introvert or an extrovert?

○ Can I talk to strangers, or do I feel uncomfortable and shy?

○ Can I make friends quickly?

○ Am I a good person to give advice to others?

○ Am I a confident person, or a negative one?

○ Am I a good problem solver?

○ Am I appreciative of other people?

○ Do I listen to and accept other's ideas and opinions?

○ Am I open to creative criticism?

- Am I responsible, and do I take responsibility for my actions?
- Am I open to new ideas and methods?
- Am I helpful and cooperative?

In these questions lie the answers to not only the type of person that you are but also the kind of leader that you can be. The answers, if given honestly and correctly, will indicate the portions of your personality that you need to work on before you become a leader.

If you are an introvert, you need to be outgoing more. If you hesitate to talk to unknown people, or if you can't make friends quickly. If you don't respond to advice and criticism well, you will need to change that.

We all have an idea of what a good leader should be like, and in analyzing ourselves, we can judge exactly how far we are from the leader that we want to become. Scrutinizing our faults and gifts, personality traits and mistakes, we can truly know ourselves, and see the kind of leader that we can become one day.

● Create a clear Vision

When you are trying to become an effective leader, it is evident that you have a goal in mind. Whether your vision is to become the next great political leader of your nation, or that your business thrives, or that your community becomes one of the most accomplished ones in your city. You will need to think and re-think every part of it vigilantly.

It's not enough to just say, "I am going to be a great leader!" if you don't know who you are going to lead, and towards what. However, if your thought is, "I want to become a part of my country's politics. For this, I will need to join my local student council and slowly work my way through the ranks to one day reach the Senate!".It will be easier to plan your course of action for the future. If you are a business person and one day want to influence your sector, your ultimate goal could be so. "I will need to motivate my employees so that they too become passionate about the company that they work for, and together, one day we can reach the top of my field!" With a vision as clear as that, it will be easy for you to follow, as well as to explain to others.

- Start Slow

Whatever your ultimate vision is in life, it is always advisable to start small. The day after your start, don't expect for thousands of people to automatically pay attention to you and follow you. That will happen eventually as you begin to proceed with your goals.

Leadership takes time, and if you are dedicated and committed enough, you will slowly reach to where you are aiming to go. If you expect a miraculous leap, all you will face is disappointment and frustration. Others will not start to follow and respect you just because you tell them to. They will do so after they have seen you strive for a result, using all your might and concentration, in achieving a goal that they too struggle for. They will watch you falter and fail, and they will see you succeed finally, and after that - when they see that you are devoted, they will begin to consider you a leader worthy of following.

So go slow; don't take the shortcut. The path to real leadership is long and tight, and to become a leader that will inspire awe and respect, you have to take the long way out.

Now that you have prepared yourself, it is time to take another step forward to becoming the leader that you can become.

Chapter 2: Habits Of Highly Effective Leaders

Great leaders are made, not born. In fact, effective leadership stems from the accumulation of good personal habits that foster certain qualities in an individual, enabling them to inspire and guide others to greater heights. In essence, anyone can learn to become a competent leader. It starts with a conscious decision to cultivate certain ways of thinking and doing things, which are then practiced until they become automated behaviors.

It Starts with You!

Before you have the capacity to competently lead others, you have to first be your own leader and take charge of your own life. As an example, let's look at the story of Carl the window cleaner:

50 year-old Carl is one of the custodians at a commercial building that housed some of the most prestigious law, tech and business firms in town. For more than a decade since he was employed, he has shown a consistent record of showing for work on-time almost every morning – save for the occasional family emergency and medical leave. Because he shows no fear for heights, he has been tasked to clean the large glass windows of the 20th floor. Every day, like clockwork, Carl would clean the same windows three times; in the morning, after lunch and before heading home. He ensures the windows are spotless, because it is his job. He does this with an understanding of how important it is for the businesses that operate in the building to project a classy image to visitors. Carl's cleaning routine is so ingrained that he does not even have to think about it. Throughout the years, his

work ethic has caught the attention of other custodians that then began emulating him.

Carl's story demonstrates what it is like to be one's own leader. He does not have a team of staff answering to him, neither is his job a glamorous one. However, Carl understands that he has a role to fulfill and a purpose to serve – as small as that purpose may be in the grand scheme of things. Hence, he took it upon himself to give it his very best every day on the job, leading by example and inspiring others to follow suit. Carl is therefore a leader.

The moral of the story is that regardless of your position on the corporate ladder – or where you are in life, for that matter – leadership skills will always serve you well.

The Personal Leadership Action Plan

By now, you should already have a basic idea of the qualities that account for good leadership. The key is to remember that becoming an effective leader is a choice, but it does involve action on one's part to cultivate the required habits and mindset.

Here is a blueprint of what you want to incorporate into your daily life when aspiring to be a better leader. Be sure to follow the simple thought exercises along the way. Spend some time to think about them, and consider jotting down your thoughts so as to make them more concrete. Also, feel free to revisit any of the points here later on, if needed.

1. Believe in and be passionate about what you do.

Effective leaders inspire others to follow along because they have a genuine passion and enthusiasm for what it is that they do. Their passion comes from the belief that they are adding value to the lives of others. If you feel that your job is insignificant and you are easily replaceable, it would help to adopt a "bigger picture outlook" and recognize that you have a service to offer.

Exercise

Consider your current job role and responsibilities. How does your job performance affect the organization's daily operations as a whole? If your job were to be removed, how would that impact the people (clients and customers) that the company serves?

2. Define your core values and live by them.

Have you ever made choices only for your decisions to have lead to a nagging feeling of unease you just couldn't shake off? You likely felt this way because you knew at the back of your mind that the decisions you made were against your core values and what you truly believed to be right.

When one's actions are at odds with their ethics, our subconscious becomes occupied with feelings of guilt and caution, hindering thoughts that are conducive to productivity and success in any endeavor. However, when our thoughts and actions are aligned with our personal values and ethics, our conscience remains clear. In addition, we will garner more trust from people when they sense integrity in our words and actions.

Exercise

Think back to a time where you made a decision or do something which you were not proud of, only for it to have haunted your conscience. Examine why it made you feel bad. Was it because you went against your personal code of ethics? Was someone or something compromised along the way? What would you have don't differently if you could go back and do it all over again? How could you make sure to not repeat this mistake again in future?

3. Maintain a positive outlook.

We do not always have control over what happens in our lives, but what we always have is control over how we chose to react to it. Someone with a positive outlook is always looking on the bright side of things.

Furthermore, optimism is infectious, and people naturally want to be around those who lift their spirits when circumstances seem less than desirable.

Exercise

Think of at least one situation where you tried to accomplish a task, but the outcome did not turn out as well as you expected. What are the good things that came out of the situation? It could be an unexpected blessing in disguise, a lesson learned or a new discovery you were able to make.

4. Know your strengths and how to utilize them.

Everyone is good at something, whether it is a technical or soft skill. Perhaps you are more knowledgeable and experienced in certain subjects than others around you. Knowing how to harness your strengths gives you an edge over others, thus making you a valuable part of a team.

Exercise

What are the technical and soft skills that you have developed over your lifetime? You may have a technical skill, such as drawing, writing, or mathematics. Maybe you are good at keeping things organized, or perhaps you are a natural conversationalist. Make a list of your strengths and think of how they come in handy at work, and in your day-to-day life. Where could you be using your talents more fully?

5. Be willing to admit your weakness and learn from mistakes.

No one is perfect, and the most successful leaders are not afraid of failure – they humbly acknowledge their shortcoming and learn from their mistakes. One of the keys to effective and respectable leadership is the willingness for a leader to communicate their weaknesses, so that others who excel at particular tasks can be appointed to the team.

Exercise

You have listed your strengths, now list your weaknesses. For the weakness that you have listed, what can you do to minimize or improve upon them? Recall a time where your weaknesses resulted in a less than desirable outcome for an assigned task. If such circumstances were to reoccur, how would you have handled them differently?

6. Learn to show, not tell.

The best leaders are those who walk the talk. You cannot inspire admiration and respect without being able to back up your claims with proactive actions.

Exercise

What value do you believe you bring to the team or company? What would you like your team or co-workers to improve upon? How can you work on modeling those qualities yourself, on a daily basis?

Chapter 3: Dealing With Self-Doubt

"I am not what has happened to me. I am what I choose to become." – Carl Jung

Before I launch into your lesson for the chapter, let me start by explaining to you how the first three chapters work. The first three stages are like our therapy session – these three chapters are where we talk about the origin of your problem and explore in depth how it affects your life. It is important to delve into this because this lack of confidence didn't simply pop up one fine morning. It developed and became deeply ingrained into your life and personality over a period of time. If you really want to change, you are going to have to understand this principle.

The steps in the chapters are clear and easy to understand. Once you have gained the understanding of the origin of your self-doubt and down-talk, I will teach you a really cool technique that will allow you to harness it and actually use your self-doubt as an improvement tool that will get you ready for further steps.

Sounds too good to be true?

Read on to find out.

For now, grab a pen and a piece of paper, you will need to take some notes on this amazing information you are about to learn. Pen and paper on hand? What are you waiting for!? Alright, let's go!

Self-doubt in small doses is actually pretty normal. But you and I both know that when self-doubt is constantly present in every decision, it can begin to interfere with your life and happiness. Let's think about it: can you think back to when your self-doubt started? What was that one important event — that exact moment when things changed for you?

Now, I know that your gut reaction is to say that you were always like this, but we've already discussed how self-doubt is acquired. Let's try to figure this one out. If you're still feeling stuck, try to pinpoint exactly which situations trigger these moments of self-doubt: public speaking, simple human interaction, thoughts that you aren't good enough, or perhaps fear of a social faux pas.

Which is it?

Now do you have it?

That single moment when everything changed?

That one person, who said something or did something that made you feel about an inch tall?

Good. Write it down.

That was Step One in eradicating self-doubt – Step Two is a little more complicated. Ready?

Forgiveness

I'm not talking about forgiving the people who might have implanted these thoughts in your mind. Actually, there is nothing to forgive since you solely have been the one to accept these thoughts as truth and no one forced them upon you. These people aren't the issue, they never were. The worst critic you had in that place, that day was you, and this forgiveness is a compassionate release that you need to extend to yourself.

Life is about more than perfection, and I know that it can be hard not to hold yourself accountable for that overwhelming feeling of inadequacy that you were drenched in that day. But you can't keep putting yourself through this. It isn't fair, and shouldn't be fair for you. So stop now! It is the only way you'll give yourself enough room to become a better person and a better leader. It's the only way you can move on.

Forgive yourself for not being perfect; that should have never been a burden you should have had in the first place.

Remember that the truest test is the test of resilience. Now that you have been able to pinpoint that particular event that robbed you of your confidence, why don't you go out and take back what is rightfully yours?

No, I'm not talking about violence – I'm talking about you taking back your thoughts. The time is now for you to prove them wrong: work hard, train harder, and become the poster-child for everything they told you that you couldn't be.

Once you have it, use your knowledge to teach someone else to do the same. A good leader inspires others to improve their skills and confidence.

4. Lessons from Leadership Vision and Purpose

I'd like to share an old story to illustrate the leadership competency of creating vision and purpose.

A medieval traveler, wandering through a city, came across a huge construction project. Near his path, he sees three stone masons, hard at work with their hammers and chisels.

"What are you doing?" asks the traveler.

"Breaking stones," grunts the first.

"Making a wall," says the second.

"Building a cathedral!" proclaims the third.

Each response tells us something about the men who responded, but it tells us even more about the leaders who led them.

When leaders create a compelling purpose and vision, something almost magical happens.

You bring out the best in your people. Which is the best stonemason? The third, and he has every reason to become better, the better he cuts those stones, the stronger his cathedral. The quicker he cuts them, the quicker it's built.

The third also enjoys the work more, because the clarity of the goal, gives him meaning and value. He enjoys the work because the end is compelling and captivating.

Additional Insights:

1. What stories in your organization illustrate your vision?

2. What stories illustrate the opposite of your vision?

3. How do you instill your desired vision into reality?

Chapter 4: Hierarchy Of Leadership

There are different levels of leadership based on the number of people one leads. You start with the first stage:

Stage 1: Being a Follower

In the beginning, no one considers you a leader. You are following another leader, just like everybody else. This is where you begin to develop your skills.

In this stage, you learn how to analyze people and how to influence them based on your analysis. You also learn about how the group works in this stage. Most people do not actively learn how their social environment works. To learn, you need to observe the people around you. To become an excellent leader, you need to have the skill of reading the motivation behind people's actions. If you know what motivates the people who surround, you can easily influence them into working together.

Stage 2: Leading Small Groups

In this stage, you begin to use your knowledge and apply it to develop your leadership skills. You try out different strategies for influencing people. You retain the skills and strategies that work and learn from those that do not.

You test these strategies while leading smaller groups. Early in your career, your goal is to gain experience in your field. The people around you will never look at you as a leader until you have the track record to prove your competence.

You will need a series of successful projects before people will begin to notice you. Once they do, you may be promoted to higher positions.

Stage 3: Being an Organizational Leader

In this stage, people around you have begun to realize that you have excellent leadership skills. You may already be in a leadership position in your group. You may also be given larger projects with more people involved.

Organizational leaders have more weight on their shoulders. However, business leaders in this group are rewarded well for their success. This is the stage where most people spend the majority of their lives. If you are an employee, this is the stage where you climb the corporate ladder. If you have your own business, this is the stage where your business grows under your leadership.

In the early parts of being an organizational leader, only a few people know about your leadership skills. You only have influence over people that you have worked with in the past. If you have a choice, you may want to bring some of these people with you in your new projects.

You can gain more attention as you are promoted to higher positions. The people who hear of your rise may ask around about you. Through word-of-mouth, your reputation will become known throughout your organization.

As this happens, you can influence more people. However, with more attention on you, your actions will be greatly scrutinized by the people in your organization. Successes will widen your reputation as a leader. However, just one misstep may undo all the positive results and fruits of your hard work. In the words of one of the most recognized leaders in business, Warren Buffett:"It takes twenty years to build a reputation, and five minutes to ruin it. If you think about that, you'll do things differently".

Stage 4: Being an Industry Leader

After years of hard work, success and failure, you may become considered as an industry leader. Industry leaders never stop learning. They never become satisfied with their skills. They start projects that affect not only their own companies, but also the whole industry. Some of them are even admired by people outside of their industries.

You will only reach this stage if you never give up on learning and reaching higher goals. Even people outside of your company will notice your leadership skills. People will look up to you because of your consistency in working hard and in reaching goals. When you are in this stage, people will listen to your every word.

Warren Buffett is an example of an industry leader. He has displayed his competence in investing money. When he talks about investing, everyone stops what he or she is doing and listens.

You may think that he was born with his leadership skills. He was not. He started out just like you and me. Over the years, he proved his value in his company and his industry. He never stopped learning. Most people his age have already retired. At 85 years old, he is still at the helm of his investing company.

Chapter 5: Going Through Leadership Challenges

People view leaders as individuals who know it all. If you are leading a company for instance, people will expect you to be the one they can always look up to. That is why in leadership, some cannot say that there is something which you do not know. Many leaders do this all the time, even when they do not have the answers their juniors are seeking. Others go to the point of living in denial because they do not want to admit that they have failed. This is not what real leadership entails though.

As a leader, one should be able to say that they do not know something, to admit that they made a mistake and to accept help and advice from other people. Honesty with yourself and with other people is very important and can make you more credible in the eyes of the people that you are leading. People expect too much from leaders but truth be told, no one knows it all. There is not a single person who can fix everything in their life. When you make it clear to other people that you do not know it all, there will be a better relationship between you, and this is what makes working together much easier.

The first step to conquering leadership is admitting that you may not have the solution to a problem. You have to constantly seek solutions in order to handle situations that your juniors do not really know how to handle, especially if you are leading an organization. What many leaders do not know is that they can easily turn such situations in their favor easily. Below are some tips that can help you out in such circumstances.

Handling Difficult Situations When You Don't Have All the Answers

Always focus on what is needed in order to fix a problem at hand. Leaders are always strategic, therefore the first thing you should do is have a problem solving strategy in place. If there is something that you can learn, you should learn it first, then proceed to solve the matter. If you are leading a group, you should take them through the situation step by step, defining the problem, the challenges the problem poses and how you can go about solving it together.

Borrow a leaf from other people's expertise and experiences. One thing that leaders should know is that the kind of problems and challenges that they face in leadership are not unique. These are issues that other leaders have dealt with in the past. You should find out how other leaders dealt with some of the issues that they faced in order to know how to handle the challenges that you will face in leadership. Constantly seek insights that can benefit you in case of challenges and difficulties.

Ask questions. A leader should always be willing to ask questions. The types of questions that you ask are also important. You need to ask probing questions that will help you to inquire deep into an issue. When you start asking more important questions, you will start getting valuable ideas and information that will help you. Do not act as an expert when fixing your team's issues. You should ask them direct questions like how they feel, if they have felt like that before and how they handled similar situations in the past.

4. Take action, even if there is a chance that you may make a mistake. In case of a problem, do not sit back and expect things to fix themselves in the end. You have to take action in whatever direction you believe is the best course. In case of any error, make sure that you have in mind several back up plans. This way, your problem solving shall still continue.

Chapter 6: The Traits Of A Good Leader, And How To Develop Them

When you ask people what determines a good leader you will often get the same answer. Many people will answer charisma. But that is a fallacy. Charisma comes from embracing the other qualities of leadership. You do not have to be charismatic to be a good leader. Instead you want to focus on the following list of 6 traits. These are the traits that all good leaders have mastered.

1.) Confidence

There are few things that people follow more than confidence. Oftentimes just acting like you know what is going on will make people instinctively trust you and follow you. If you do not have confidence all you need to do is fake it until you develop this ability. Confidence comes from being willing to make a stand for your beliefs. It is ok to be wrong, simply acknowledge the mistake and move on. That is what confident people do. They know they will make mistakes, but they learn from them. They are willing to be the first to try knowing that the first to try has an advantage in practically anything.

If you have a problem with confidence you need to try to fake it. Practice a speech in front of a mirror until you have it down to a point where you can also fake confidence. Eventually you will notice that your fake confidence is turning into the real thing.

2.) Delegation

The ability to delegate is a rare talent. Most people are unable to hand things over, and instead run themselves ragged trying to accomplish an impossible workload. This is not the path of leadership. A true leader not only has no difficulty assigning work, they also are familiar with the strengths and weaknesses of their team. This lets them make sure that when they delegate they assign it to the best person possible for the job. This makes the leader look good, but will also let their follower receive acknowledgment. A true leader does not mind sharing in the spoils of victory.

A problem with delegation is easy to fix, but hard to eliminate. The next thing that you can delegate do so. This can be as simple as asking your spouse to wash the dishes. You have to practice delegation. Work your way up with tasks. Always remember to analyze who would be best to perform the task. This will maximize your team's results.

3.) Commitment

To many wannabe leaders are unwilling to perform at the level that they expect of others. You have to be committed to be a leader. A true leader leads from the front. They show by their own personal example what they expect of others. When you lead from the front your followers will follow you to the ends of the earth. A follower should follow. A leader should lead. Always make sure that you are more dedicated to success than anyone else who follows you.

Commitment is one of the hardest leadership skills to develop. You have to learn to be able to force yourself to do things that you do not want to do. Some people find success in pretending to be their own boss. They will assign themselves jobs that must be completed, and then perform as much as they can. A good place to start is by making changes in your personal life. If you are overweight, start losing weight. If you are unhealthy, change your habits. Make sure that your personal life reflects the qualities that you believe a leader should have.

4.) Creativity

When many people hear that creativity is important they remove themselves from the running of being a leader. This is unfortunate as creativity is easy. Being creative means that you can overcome obstacles that are put in front of you. You can outcompete other leaders because you have new ideas that you are constantly putting into practice. A true leader makes fake leaders follow the path that they have blazed.

Being creative is a simple 3 step process. First you have to decide what your goal is. Figure out where the finish line is at. Then make a decision about how to move closer to the goal. Then analyze your progress. If you didn't move closer to the goal, come up with another idea to try. If you didn't make the progress you wanted all you need to do is to try something else. Then keep trying until you reach your goal. You may go through dozens of ideas. But you will find that each idea that you try gives you more information about the situation. This makes it easier and easier for each new idea to be better than the last.

5.) Ability to Inspire

Having the ability to inspire simply means that you can get higher performance from people than they are capable of getting from themselves. The classical view of a leader is someone who is good at speeches. That view thinks that the ability to fire someone up is how you inspire. This is true, but only to a point. There are other ways to inspire. These include a word of encouragement at the right time, the ability to see when something is wrong, or even just setting clear expectations.

A great way to learn to inspire is to pit your followers against another leader and their followers. Human beings by nature are competitive. Setting up a game or friendly competition is a great way to motivate others to increase performance. Keep raising the goals and you will be surprised how much can be accomplished. Always make sure that the goals are reasonable though, as otherwise people can become disheartened.

6.) Communication

Most wannabe leaders do not have the ability to communicate. Their communication style is limited to a single type. The majority of them use anger, passion, or even yelling as their preferred communication style. This is fine for some followers. But there are many different ways to communicate. The best leaders use the style of communication that is best for each of their followers. They may have to speak to them separately. This lets the leader use the best type of communication for each follower, and helps to maximize their response.

If you have problems with communicating it can help to spend time thinking about how best to talk to each person. You may find that certain people respond to approaching them with drive or passion. Others may be best approached by simple check in every now and then to see how they are handling their responsibilities. The best way to learn different communication styles is to experiment. Ask your followers how they like to be approached. If you are a good leader in other ways they will tell you the best way to speak to them.

Chapter 7: Communication And Humility

"There is nothing noble in being superior to your fellow man; true nobility is being superior to your former self." – Ernest Hemingway

A true leader remembers where his roots lie. He remembers the hard struggle to get where he currently is and doesn't lose sight of the fact that he was not always a leader. Humility is what helps him to do this. You may wonder how self-awareness comes into the picture but it is a vital part of becoming a great leader. You cannot measure the progress that you have made unless you are able to clearly see the steps that took you there. When people are aware of self, they know their strengths and are not afraid to face up to their weaknesses. Being self-aware means that they don't kick themselves for mistakes, or blame others. What great leaders do is use mistakes as stepping stones to the future and turns them into learning opportunities.

Richard Branson – a great industrial leader of our time – says, "Anyone who says they have never made a mistake has just made one." He acknowledges that he makes mistakes and is very self-aware. His businesses are growing and making a lot of money because he is a kick ass boss who isn't afraid of his errors. He admits to making many mistakes each day and by being this humble is able to investigate his errors and find better solutions. Being humble allows him to avoid fear or negativity caused by his mistakes. Mistakes only become negative when you allow them to be overwhelmingly difficult. Instead of allowing mistakes to be negative, examine the mistakes and use them to learn.

If a man was to try and sweep the road with the wind blowing the dirt in the opposite direction to his brush, simple physics and examination of what is happening will tell him to turn around and sweep in the opposite direction if he wants to achieve his aim. In the same way, examination of errors helps a great leader to approach problems in a different way and discover which ways work better than the attempts that failed.

Communication is everything when it comes to leadership. If you make errors and insist on blaming others, you gain little respect. There are some people who consider themselves to be leaders when what they actually do is pass the buck when it comes to apportioning blame. Leaders don't do that. They communicate with all involved and find out why things went wrong, but they don't do so to apportion blame. They do so to motivate their team or their workers to do better next time and to stay motivated.

If you have ever worked for someone who blames others, you will understand that this is counter-productive and helps no one. However, an effective communicator is able to put all the pieces together and work out what approach can be used in order to avoid mistakes in the future, rather than concentrating on the negative aspects that make others feel like failures. Part of the communication process is being able to tackle team members and find out how things can change to get around hurdles or even over them.

Imagine a team member who trips during a race and knocks over a hurdle. A good leader will be able to look at the whole situation rather than making the team member feel like an idiot. He will be able to evaluate risks and will be able to make that team member feel enthused to try a different way. He doesn't demotivate. He fills people who work for him with enthusiasm and motivation. In a well-known quotation by Bill Gates, he mentions "any tool that enhances communication has profound effects in terms of how people can learn from each other and how they can achieve the kind of freedoms they are interested in." This quotation shows you that great leaders need to learn to understand the people who are involved in all matters that serve the purpose of the leader. By making himself available to communicate at all levels, he leads because he fosters mutual respect and people respond well to that kind of behavior.

Effective leaders are not afraid to let their views be known, but have the common sense to know that they are not the only people with views. They are not blind-sighted by their inability to listen. You may not be aware of it but communication does not just mean talking. It means listening and the kind of listening that a great communicator does as part of their everyday activities helps to give them stature, as well as gaining the respect of others. When you are unable to listen and fully analyze situations, you lose control of them. Thus, listening and learning is a far more effective habit to foster.

Great leaders are effective speakers because they enthuse others. What they say has substance and meaning to all who are listening because it's aimed to be effective. It doesn't ignore anyone who is part of the equation. Thus, great communication has to be one of the most important habits of a kick ass leader. Humility allows that communicator to recognize what problems are and how to rectify them to the satisfaction of all concerned, rather than just thinking of the smaller picture of short term gain for himself.

Chapter 8: Always Think About Number #1

"Be "One" Even If You're Last"

The point of business in most circumstances is to make money. You know that and I know that.

You start a business to make money. You work at a business to make money. Now granted nonprofits and charitable organizations may have their own concepts, but for the sake of the point here, we are talking about for profit companies.

So let me ask you this...

Do you want the business that you own or work for to succeed?

I mean really think about it.

I'm almost 110% sure if you own your own business you said YES right away in your head.

But what if you're a manager of a fast food restaurant, a mechanic, nurse, accountant, or some other field where you work for someone else? Do you care if the company succeeds? Or do you only care that every two weeks (maybe more or less) you have a fresh off of the press paycheck with your name on it?

Be honest with yourself.

The point here is that to be a positive leader, you must lead with positivity no matter if you're a contract employee, an intern, or on the retirement track within a company.

And to lead with positivity, you must great a "One" company.

I truly want you and your company to succeed.

So to be successful in the present, you must create a "One" atmosphere.

Ready? Let's begin.

What's "One" all about? And I know you might be saying, "Hey this Chris guy just told me last chapter that it's not about me, what gives?"

So my theory of "One" is this:

For a business to be successful for today and tomorrow, through the ups and downs, you must be UNITED!

Ding Ding Ding! We have a Winner!

See it's like this, if you have employees that are just bodies, cashing paychecks, and flying low enough under the radar to not get fired, how are they representing your brand?

In a United or "One" company, each and every employee shares the Mission, Vision, and represents the Brand.

Let me explain.

If you own your own business, you probably have an image that you want to keep intact or to be represented in a certain way. But if I work for you and have no idea how I should represent your brand, we are now a company of "Two."

If you have a specific vision, but I don't see it, how am I helping?

And what if you want me to wear a fancy company branded shirt while on service calls, and I don't, am I representing the brand?

For a business to grow, you must be willing to share the mission statement, share the vision of the owners or company, and express how the brand should be represented.

Here is a more in depth example:

The company that you own is a Bakery:

I work for you.

There are 35 employees altogether.

We all know the Mission of your company.

We all know the Vision of the company.

We all know why the company was created.

We all know how we should represent the brand / company.

We all participate in meetings and discussions.

We all are treated equally no matter our titles or pay scales.

We all get to speak and contribute to marketing ideas.

We all get to know about any new ideas and products.

We all get to know how each item is created and tested.

- We all get to try our own products and or services.

Can you feel the difference?

See when you create a "One" company, everyone compliments everyone else.

If a customer has a complaint, each employee can talk to the person as they know how each item is created.

If you ask me to work an extra hour, I will go out of my way to help because I am not treated like an outsider, but as a member of a united company.

When I get ready for work each day, I take the time to look my best, because your company deserves the best.

I interact with my fellow co-workers as we all share the same common goals within the company.

We all desire success for this company, because we are not just numbers on a time card, we are valued employees!

See that is the difference!

I love it when I go to a business or company and just sit and watch them.

I listen to the people, the employees, and the atmosphere.

It doesn't take long to see if the business is a "One" company or a bunch of paycheck hunters!

When I call my wireless carrier and I ask about my plan or something, I want to feel like the person on the phone truly cares about me as a customer.

When I take my family to a nice dinner, I want to know that the cooks are not dropping my food on the floor because they care about the quality and because they respect the company as a whole.

When I get me car fixed, I want to know that the person putting new tires on my car checks to make sure my lug nuts are tight as if it was their family driving away.

If you want to grow your business, as a friend I'm telling you, create a "One" atmosphere within your company, your team, or group. If it's you and a partner, get on the same page like yesterday.You need to know that if you were not at work, the "One" company atmosphere is unbreakable.

If you want to call yourself a Positive Leader, create a positive environment!

Have meetings with the janitor, the mail clerk, the CEO, the receptionist, and anyone else that you can.

Be the listening tree. Let people express their concerns, fears, and wishes for the company. You never know where the next big idea may come from.

I actually go out of my way to ask people about their ideas for the company.

You can do the same thing.

If your employees feel like they are a vital voice for your company, I can almost guarantee you that your employees will represent your company with respect and dignity!

They will work harder, smarter, and make you more money!

But all profits and success aside, when you work in a "One" company, everyone wants to help their partner in the next cubicle or chair or department.

Everyone has a voice and a purpose. When employees answer calls, or create products, or perform services, it's no longer just about a paycheck, it's about them being a part of something bigger.

As a Positive Leader, you must start the movement towards a company or business of "One."

Want to know how?

Start planting seeds of success, positivity, leadership, and love today, so that the company that you work for or operate, can grow tomorrow!

Key Notes:

1. Assess the company that you work for… is it a company of "One"?

2. Do the employees around you only care about a paycheck?

3.   If you asked someone in the hall what is the mission of the company, do they know?

4.   The most successful companies I believe are the ones who stand together, as "One"!

Chapter 9: How To Add Value To Other People's Life

To add value to others is a way of creating success not just for a leader only but for everyone. Adding value to others is also another thing all successful leaders have in common. In the process of adding value to other people's life, you also become more valuable to them. Adding value to other people's life is a way to make them believe in you. People respect those who add value to them. This book on its own is a way of adding value to other people's life. Many will read it and become better equipped for leadership adding meaning to their lives. For me on the other hand I possibly might get response that will inspire me to write more books to benefit everyone. For a leader to add value to others, they must first add value to themselves. It could be reading to become a better leader or developing an attribute peculiar to a leader. As a leader, you must connect, uplift and enrich the lives of others to succeed. Leaders who add value, build better relationship with everyone around them learning about what they find valuable to them so as to lead them successfully.

Value is whatever has the chance of making you better in any way or achieve what you want. The job of today is purely to create value and deliver it to other people. Leaders who add value to others have to trust in their people before this trust can be reciprocated. They serve others instead of expecting to be served. We add value to others when we make ourselves more valuable to others. Encouraging other people adds value to them. Try to get the best out of people by encouraging them to be the best they can be. This will inspire them to take their own risks and add their own value to the world. In other to add value to other people, you have to without dispute have added value to yourself. You have to have something before you can give it. Developing your own values precedes any other thing.

For a leader to add value to others, he has to have precedence to cater for what people need and not want. The need to feel important and help other people meet these needs. The first step to being successful or successfully adding value to other people's life starts with you asking what would be of greater value to other people. For you to know if you are really adding value to other people's life, you have to know that whatever you are making is adding to someone, that you are doing your best in the situation at hand and that everything I am doing is with a sense of love. Adding value could be in form of an emotional connection. Falling in love with someone is a way of adding value to the person's life. They get to know what it feels like to love.

This process is one that changes an individual's perspective. The welfare of other people begin to matter to you hereby not only contributing to your success but also to that of other people. This give existence a much deeper meaning. Adding value to other people's life starts with just one person rather than a crowd. It starts from you adding value to that one person sitting beside you at the moment be it a friend, acquaintance, spouse, siblings and so on. Like a saying; little drops of water make mighty ocean. If everyone adds value to all those around them, then there would be little work left for the leaders to do. You succumbing to receiving value from those around you not only helps them but also helps you too. All the same never see adding value to others as bartering. It is more of a means of helping the world and not your individual self. You never know how or when you will benefit from it but you certainly will. No matter how we add value, it must be genuine and positively helpful.

WAYS TO ADD VALUE TO OTHERS

Ways to add value to other people starts with u.

Know your own abilities first. What you are capable of doing. It is these abilities that will allow you to add value to other people.

Start by doing what you love and enjoy. Doing things you love not only makes you better at it but it also make using them as a tool to add value a more natural experience.

Your job should be a means of adding value to others. Your job should be a limelight, pathway to giving value to other people's life.

By just being there for someone in their time of need is a way of adding value to their life. You make them feel loved. Being loved is a value on its own.

Make something that will be useful to other people rather than yourself.

In moments of need, you could add value to someone by simply inspiring them to take necessary actions.

Be of help to others in every little way you can. It could be as simple as helping someone carry an extra set of grocery bags to their doorstep. Helping is helping.

You could add value by showing someone how something is done or even by showing them a better or faster way to go about something. This could be as simple as putting a video on YouTube to help someone herby adding value to them.

You could also add value by providing someone with a new perspective or by giving them an idea to help them become better individuals.

A leader doing what should be done in the right way is a great way to add value to everyone around them. Their life itself becomes a means of adding value.

If you have a choice of two or more paths, always choose the one that allows you to add the most value. This will keep you in alignment with your true purpose in life and will, ultimately, bring you greater happiness and greater reward. Failure should be a charge to you to forge ahead. Failure will only make you a better person. Leadership is about how much value we have added to other people and the effect it has on them.

Adding value to people's life make them think differently. Once you can successfully influence someone to have a better opinion of something you have added value to their lives. A person who influences someone will always add value to other people's life. Helping people achieve their goal is one of the greatest way of adding value to other people's life.

OUTCOMES OF ADDING VALUE TO OTHERS

Adding value brings joy

Adding value brings back humanity

Adding value adds color to life

Adding value make you better equipped to be a leader

Adding value makes life more meaningful.

Adding value makes you a better influencer

Adding value makes you successful.

Adding value attracts people to want to follow you.

Providing value to others give purpose to our own life as well. And by knowing the ways to do this most especially for those you love and that are close to you will give value to your own life as well. What needs to be done to optimize adding value to other people's life is to continually make every day count by adding as much value as you can. Albert Einstein said, 'Only a life lived for others is worth living.' This makes living for others a way of adding value. Adding value to others makes you a better person and every little way of adding value counts. The reward of adding value is much greater than the effort put into doing so. This makes adding value to others a win-win scenario. What you are doing for someone else is actually beneficial to you. Life is strange like that! I will like to finish up with a quote from Brendon Burchard he said "part of adding value is helping people reconnect with some emotional side of their lives. In any situation, bring back the humanity, the emotion, the color, the flare, the joy, the vibrancy, the real hues of human emotion and you will go to a level of adding value that most people will never replicate."

Chapter 10: Practicing Leadership

To practice being a leader, it is important to understand when it is important to step in and when it is best to step aside. Here are a few suggestions to help you determine the best times to assert yourself as a leader.

Know a problem when you see it

As a leader, it is important to know your team well enough to understand when then can handle tasks by themselves and when you need to get involved. To best practice this art, it is important to know what your specific talents are and where you are best suited to let others handle a situation. Likewise, it is important to understand the warning signs of trouble for members of your team individually so you can step in when it is required. A good leader can prevent problems from occurring and avert disaster without anyone else even knowing.

Perform under pressure

As a new leader, it is important that sometime soon after you step into your new role you find yourself in a situation where you can prove your chops to your new team. Depending on your specific situation, this may be difficult to come by and as such you may need to nudge it along a little. If this is the case, then it is important to find an issue that the team is dealing with and make it known that you will find a way to deal with it regardless of the specifics. Good places to start are with the physical conditions of your team's space, the extension of a difficult deadline or a commitment to solve a particular interpersonal problem. The important thing to remember is that it should be something that has a real impact on your team's day to day experience (within reason).

In this case, it is important to pick an issue that is major enough for the attempt to be noticed, but minor enough that you can handle it either by yourself of with buy-in from the group that you can predict and prepare for. After you have taken care of your chosen issue it is important to go out of your way not to bring it to your team's attention. If they have the time to discover to discover your success for themselves, they will be more appreciative of it. After you have achieved your first victory it is important to snowball your success into a new direction. You have the momentum you need; all you need to do now is run with it.

Have a plan

As the leader, it is important that you understand both the micro and macro goals that your team is trying to accomplish. Even if you aren't actively engaged in the completion of a particular project, it is important that you are aware of what is going on with that project and more importantly how it relates to the larger goals you team is trying to accomplish. It is fine to let your team work largely autonomously on smaller projects, but they rely on you to know the way the wind is blowing at that is something you cannot leave to chance lest your team lose an even keel and drift off course.

Having a plan doesn't mean being inflexible to the point of being rigid. Instead, it means having an idea of where the team is headed for the future. It is perfectly fine for your plan to change as your team changes, as long as you have an idea of where the team is going and why. If you aren't sure what your plan should be, start by taking a look at your team. Consider each member of the team and how you would like for them to grow in the next six months. Think about their strengths and weaknesses and how they could best be maximized for the good of the whole. Finally, consider how you can help them get there. Do this for each member of your team and see how they can best complement one another. Congratulations, you now have a plan.

Share your plan

Once you have a plan in mind it is important to share it with the entire team, get their feedback and ensure that everyone buys into your vision for the future. Once a team has accepted you as their leader and bought-in to your plan for the future you can expect them to stop working for you and begin to work with you to accomplish mutually beneficial goals. An effective leader can ensure that their team meets all of their goals, a good leader ensures that their team wants to meet all of their goals. While it can be difficult to present a plan to an untested team and ask for feedback, this is a crucial step in getting your team to stop acting like a group of people who work together and start behaving like a proper team. This is the mark of a real leader.

When To Argue And When To Let It Go

We've already taken a look at how to handle disagreements and how to deal with annoying co-workers, but sometimes you need to ask yourself whether an issue is really worth bothering with in the first place. If you find yourself frequently drawn into conflicts and disagreements – or having to sort them out between two or more of your team members – it may be time to consider whether you are granting too much time to the wrong kinds of issue. Consider the following points when you sense an argument brewing at work.

Sometimes it's better to let someone make a minor mistake by themselves, as long as they have the ability to clear up the mess! Is a member of your team insistent that they be allowed to do something a certain way, even though it is plain to other people that they are setting themselves up for a fall? One way to handle such a situation is to grant them the chance to teach themselves a lesson. If possible, tell them that you disagree with how they want to handle the scenario, but that you want to let them learn from their own experiences. Take a deep breath and let them make their own mistakes. Note that you should never do this if the stakes are high, but that allowing someone to make their own errors can be a valuable teaching tool.

Of course, if it turns out that they were right, don't be too proud to admit that they have done a good job. Be humble!

Don't take the fall for someone else.

Although a good leader protects their team to some extent and accepts ultimate responsibility for their outcomes, there is little sense in risking your own reputation for the sake of keeping the peace and going along with a suggestion you feel to be wrong. If someone else's stubborn nature will cost you personally, state your case and then put your foot down.

Ask yourself whether the issue will cease to matter within a week or month.

If the answer is 'No, it won't matter to anyone,' then it probably isn't worth arguing about. Smooth things over as quickly as possible and move onto more important topics. Your time is a valuable commodity, and it makes no sense to argue about petty issues when you have bigger priorities on which to focus. Model this attitude for your team, and they will learn where to direct their own energies.

Sometimes you have to let other people disagree – from separate rooms.

Sometimes it is appropriate to let two of your team members engage in healthy disagreement. However, if they start calling one another names or dragging up issues from the past, it's time to step in and force a truce. This may require you to send one off to engage in an unrelated work task, or even to ask them to sit in separate rooms for a while. If your office atmosphere is informal and the issue is relatively petty, try to gently point out that they are silly to argue this particular point. This may be enough to help them realize that their time would be better spent elsewhere.

Try to foresee issues that may cause conflict ahead of time, so you can anticipate how best to diffuse the situation. For instance, if you know that two of your team members are likely to get into a disagreement at a particular meeting, you could have a discreet conversation with them both prior to the event and state that whilst you respect that they have a difference of opinion, you are expecting that they will both agree to act like mature adults and share in their commitment to act in the best interests of the company.

Consider the context.

If you catch yourself feeling especially irritable one day for no apparent reason, stay on your guard so as to make sure you don't get into unnecessary arguments. As a rule, do not argue when you are unusually busy, when you are especially tired, or first thing on a Monday morning - this will set an unpleasant tone for the rest of the week.

Chapter 11: The Honest Leader

It is difficult if not altogether impossible to trust a person who is deceptive. People want to depend on someone whom they know will not trick them into doing something against their will or leading them into a trap. It is for this reason that a leader should be honest.

Being honest to your team shows that you are a professional, even during times when the truth is not pleasant, the leader should nevertheless practice transparency. The team will be grateful for that and would in fact strive to work harder. Moreover, by displaying honesty as a virtue that you uphold in the team, the other members would be encouraged to be fair and honest with each other as well.

Be careful not to mistake honesty for candidness. You must also identify and take into full consideration the social culture of the people with whom you are conversing, for being too direct is often equated to being rude in many societies. Create that balance of being just as sensitive as you are honest, for that is what makes a great leader.

How to Become One:

To become an honest leader, you must strive to be authentic. While it is challenging to be truly honest and stand for what you believe in, it is this overcoming this challenge that makes a leader great. Make the decision to be honest each day by keeping the following strategies in mind:

Follow through with your commitments. If you commit to doing something, you should make it a point to stick to it. You can only gain the respect of others when they know that you are the kind of person they can depend on. A person who abandons their responsibilities when the going gets tough definitely does not have what it takes to become a great leader. This being said, you should also know when to say no. If you know without a doubt that something is beyond you or your team's scope, you should be honest about it instead of taking on the role and ending up with a poor output.

Owning up to your weaknesses. Dishonest people have the habit of covering up their weaknesses because they feel embarrassed or threatened by them. They would even put their team at risk just to save themselves and avoid the confrontation. This may be hard to do, but strive to be honest about your own mistakes to the rest of the team. They will be more considerate and respectful towards you when they know that you are aware of your transgressions and that you are making an effort to improve.

Be tactful. Trouble only stems out of one's being too honest when the wrong words are chosen to express honesty. An honest leader is someone who ensures that the feedback he or she is giving is constructive and will inspire that person to do better. Great leadership is when you can address the situation in an honest and professional way and not let your own anger get in the way of your team's progress.

Lastly, be specific in relaying a message to others. Do not treat the rest of the team as mind readers who can pick up passive aggressive statements and use these to improve themselves. You can be specific without hurting anyone's feelings by starting your statements by applying the sandwich method, which is to point out something positive, followed by constructive feedback, then another positive aspect. This will help you to stay honest without lowering the morale of your team.

Chapter 12: Communicating Like A True Leader

Having good communication skills is a must if you want to become a leader. Having this tool will greatly improve your ability to motivate and influence others.

Communicate in an organized manner

You need to make sure that the information presented is organized. Even if you have someone writing your speeches for you, it would still be wise to check them over. This will ensure that your listeners will understand what you are saying.

There will be many instances when you will need to communicate with the group. Before every meeting you should mentally organize all of the topics you will be going over. If you have trouble remembering any of these topics, you should write them down. Also, try to avoid straying from your prepared topics. All of these steps may seem unnecessary, but it will ensure that you do not make a mess out of the meeting.

Modulate your voice

A well-modulated voice can be a valuable asset to leaders. If you have noticed, presidents usually have deep voices. Even women who run for the position try to speak in the same manner. You should modulate your voice in the same way if you want to become an effective leader. You should practice speaking with a slightly deepened voice, but at the same time make it sound loud and assertive. Although having these qualities when you speak could be a good thing, if you try too hard to make your voice sound this way it may come across as unnatural and will end up being less effective.

People, in general associate a deep voice as a leadership characteristic. You should use this kind of voice regardless when speaking in public. Using it in the right context will create an image of authority.

Create communication personas

There are times when you need to appear as an authority and times when you need to appear as a friend to the people you are interacting with. As the head of a company for example, you may need to appear in a jolly mood when facing investors and customers of the business. When the time comes to discipline an employee's faulty work, you may need to put on a more serious face.

A leader needs to create personas to adapt to these situations. Most leaders develop these personas over a lifetime of experience. It is possible to deliberately create these personas by practicing them.

You should, at the very least, have a happy and a serious persona. Your whole face should change with these personas. It may sound strange, but an effective way to create these faces is by changing your facial expressions in front of a mirror. This is important because if you get it wrong you will fail to create a convincing expression.

Anyone can fake a smile to appear happy, but your eyes are what show your true emotions. When practicing this you must make sure that your whole face cooperates. You should be able to make your eyes look happy at will.

You should also practice your serious face. This persona will come into play when you are giving important orders and instructions to the people you lead. Some people naturally have happy facial expressions. This is not always a bad thing, but when it is time to be serious, having happy facial expressions may give people the impression that you can be taken advantage of. Similar to your happy face, your serious face will be shown in your eyes.

Chapter 13: On Leadership Qualities

Many leaders have the capability to succeed, but a small percentage excel to the level of being remarkable. If you wish to be in the lines of the greatest of the great, make certain you exemplify all the qualities cited below always. It is not easy, yet the prize can truly be phenomenal.

Accountability

Exceptional leaders accept responsibility over the performance of everyone, including their personal actions. They keep an eye on altogether outstanding matters, check on every employee, and observe the efficiency of established procedures and policies.

When everything is going fine, they praise their followers, but when problems rise, they recognize them swiftly, seek the way out of these problems and urge things to reverse.

Awareness

There remains a variance between administration and workers, bosses and workforce. Leaders comprehend the makeup of this variance and agree to embrace it. It forms their appearance, actions, and communication. Hence, they conduct themselves within a manner which sets them separately from their personnel, not in a way which suggests they are better compared to others, instead in a manner which promotes an attitude of being goal oriented over everything that is taking place in their group.

Confidence

Not solely are the unsurpassed leaders self-assured, but their self-confidence is contagious. Employees remain naturally pulled to them, ask their guidance and, as a result, feel additionally confident. They understand that their thoughts, opinions, as well as strategies, are knowledgeable and the product of plentiful hard labor.

But once proven incorrect, they accept responsibility, and quickly act to make the conditions better within their power.

Decisiveness

All leads must make tough choices, which goes with the work. They appreciate that within certain circumstances, difficult and timely decisions should be made in the best interest of the whole organization. These decisions require flexibility, authority and conclusiveness that may not please everyone. Extraordinary leads do not hesitate within such states and they also distinguish when not to proceed, but in its place foster concerted decision-making.

Empathy

Extraordinary leads give praise in public, while also addressing difficulties in private. The top leaders give employees concrete direction regarding challenges, being continuously on guard for answers to every glitch in order to nurture the lasting success of the group.

Rather than make things subjective when they meet problems, or putting blame towards individuals, leads look towards constructive resolutions and concentrate on proceeding forward.

Focus

Extraordinary leads plan in advance and are completely organized. They consider multiple situations and the likely impacts of their choices, while seeing viable replacements and creating plans, besides strategies, which are all beleaguered toward victory.

Once ready, they start strategies, procedures and practices to facilitate high routine to be tangible, straightforwardly defined and checked. They convey their tactics to important players, as well as have emergency plans should last-minute circumstances require a fresh direction, which they habitually do.

Honesty

Strong heads treat persons how they wish to remain treated. They stay extremely principled and trust that uprightness, effort and dependability form the basis of achievements. They symbolize these standards so openly that no worker doubts their honesty at all. They distribute information freely and avoid manipulating their followers.

Inspiration

When you put together all the listed qualities of the preeminent leader, what arises is an image of the really inspiring lead, who communicates undoubtedly, concisely and regularly, and in so doing, motivates each member to offer their finest.

They test their members by putting high, but possible expectations and standards, and at that juncture, give them the provision, tools, preparation and leeway to follow those objectives and be the exemplary employees they could possibly become.

Optimism

The extremely best leads are a source of optimistic energy and this they communicate effortlessly. They remain accommodating and truly concerned regarding the welfare of other people. They continually appear to hold a solution, as well as always know what to say to motivate and assure.

They evade personal censure and negative thinking, instead looking for means to increase consensus, as well as get persons to function together professionally and efficiently as a group.

Chapter 14: Leadership Examples And Scenarios

Stories and examples of successful leaders are by far one of the most efficient ways of learning about leadership. It's a topic that has been studied and researched for many years. Even though leadership has been talked about since the time of Plato, the first serious study tracks back to 1920s. This included the first leadership theory also known as trait theory. This study attempted to identify the common characteristics of leaders.

Without getting into too much detail about the history of leadership, I'd like to give a few examples of leaders who have been able to turn around the situations of organizations using the positive attitudes described in the section before.

Eastman Kodak

In the 70s Eastman Kodak, which is commonly known as the company Kodak, faced a situation where even though revenues were growing, the costs of machines were growing just as fast. Making it tough for the company to maintain healthy profit levels. The company had about $ 1 billion in revenues, however in 1984 Kodak has to write off the inventory of nearly $ 40 million. This was raising serious concerns for the company. The newly appointed general manager, Chuck Trowbridge knew the change had to be brought quickly to turn the situation around.

To do so, he was engaging with the key personnel in the company, especially the manufacturing and engineering head, Bob Crandall.

The goal Chuck Trowbridge and Bob Crandall wanted to achieve was to turn the organization into a less bureaucratic and more decentralized organization. In doing so, they wanted Kodak to become a world class manufacturing operation. The biggest challenge was that the organization norm and culture was completely the opposite. Bringing about such a change did not come easy.

To start off, Chuck and Bob set up a weekly meeting with their direct reports to talk about the key issues and challenges being faced on a daily basis. Also once a month Bob held meetings with 80 to 100 of his staff members to discuss absolutely anything they felt would enhance the operational performance of the department.

The key point to emphasize was that Chuck and Bob were trying to align everyone internally with the vision they have developed to save the company in falling into a pit. To engage and align external people they held a weekly meeting with the biggest suppliers also.

Written communications were streamlined to allow employees the opportunity to ask questions anonymously to Bob Crandall and his top managers. This program was called "Dialogue Letters" where employees were guaranteed a response. Another visible and effective approach was the use of charts in hallways in the building areas, they reported the quality, cost and delivery results of each product.

All of this led to significant improvements within a matter of six months. Defects per unit went from 30 to 0.3. Over a three-year period, costs on a product line went down nearly 24%. Deliveries on schedule increased from 82% to 95%. Inventory levels dropped by 50%, though the volume of products kept rising. In 1988, when productively measured in "units per manufacturing employee" was evaluated it has almost doubled.

Aligning people to the vision is a powerful tool used by the effective leader to bring about massive change. Had the efforts been spent on hiring the right people for the key positions, chances are, results would have continued to show a downward trend for Eastman Kodak.

American Express

Another great example is American Express. This demonstrates how leadership can setup great direction to bring about the change they envision. When Lou Gerstner became the President of Travel Related Services (TRM) at American Express, the company was facing fierce competition from MasterCard and Visa. The highly competitive nature of the industry was taking its toll as banks were ready to issue credit cards through competitors.

American Express was faced with one of the most difficult situations in its 130 years history as profit margins dropped and growth become difficult.

Lou Gerstner envisions the company to be dynamic and growing enterprise, with a wide range of products and services. The traditional belief that was common in American Express was to heavily dependent on one product i.e. the green card. Furthermore, people believed that this product had limited potential for growth and innovation.

Within a few weeks of his appointment, Gerstner brought key members of the organization together and started questioning their principles by which business was conducted. Also, to move quickly toward a more entrepreneurial culture, intelligent risk taking was rewarded, and bureaucracy was discouraged in business. To further enhance the entrepreneurial skills of teams people were given a higher degree of top management folks, graduate management programs were introduced, and recognition and reward standard were improved (especially in customer service areas).

As simple as these actions may sound, they were geared to align people with the vision of having a dynamic and growing enterprise, with a broad range of products and services. The initiatives resulted in Amex cards being issued in 29 currencies (as opposed to only 11 a decade earlier). The company expanded its products and services to new markets. In 1981, TRM combined its card and travel-service abilities to offer corporate clients a unified system to monitor and control travel expenses. By 1988, the company has become the fifth largest direct-mail merchant in the USA. Other new products included the 90-days insurance on all purchases made with AmEx cards. The company also newer processing technology for billing and providing more convenient monthly statements for customers that reduced billing costs by 25%.

The results were phenomenal; American Express increased its net income by 500%, over a ten-year period. The business outperformed many high-tech companies, with a return on equity of 28% in 1988.

Procter and Gamble

Another great example is of Procter and Gambles' associate general manager, Richard Nicolosi, who used motivation to turn around the company. Faced with fierce competition the company was rapidly losing market share in the 1970s.

Internally, P&G was challenged with bureaucratic and internal warfare. People within the organization had formed two major groups of technical and commercial individuals respectively. Competing with one another on cost savings and functional goals, P&G found it difficult to grow and regain its market share.

As soon as Richard Nicolosi came to his new position, he started emphasizing the need to being more market-focused instead of cost savings and functional goals. He began monthly and weekly meetings with his leading teams and started categorizing them into major brand groups. Responsibilities were moved towards these teams encouraging them to be innovative and creating new ideas for product developments. This engaged people and shifted the focus towards development rather than competing internally. Staff morale was uplifted this way, as there was something new on which to focus.

In addition, new motivational teams were formulated to communicate new vision about products and inputs from team members were welcomed. Nicolosi, along with board members, emphasized the idea "each of us is a leader" during meetings and company events. This helped create a new environment entity-wide and engaged everyone towards a more exciting future of the company.

One of P&Gs products, ultra pampers, in 1985 increased market share from 40% to 58% and profitability from break-even to positive. Within a few months the company's overall brand great by 150% in market share. P&G further went on to establish new recognition and reward programs. By 1988 revenues were up 40%

over a four year period and profits were up 68%, and this happened despite the continued increase in competition in the market.

Change brought on top

Senior leadership can turn things around, if they use tools such as motivation, aligning people with company vision and providing direction. A common theme noticed in all of these examples was the increased communication with the major members or teams and decentralization of business structures. The results of these simple efforts brought about a massive change and turned company performance around 180 degrees.

Chapter 15: How To Influence People?

One of the manifestations of good leadership is the leader's ability to influence other people. This chapter will discuss some of the most effective strategies on how to become a more influential leader.

Have a genuine interest on other people

Your level of influence is based largely on your ability to connect to those who are around you. Do you take time to be genuinely interested on what the others are saying? Show your members that you are genuinely interested in them. This shows that you sincerely and genuinely care for their feelings and thoughts, as well as value their contribution to the group. Once you make them feel this way, you can easily influence them to follow your lead.

Build a harmonious relationship

Make your members feel comfortable when you are around. Instead of establishing hate and fear, you should make your followers feel that you are the kind of leader whom they can easily approach. Socialize with them from time to time. When it's break time, try to talk to them or share stories. This is a huge help in instilling trust within your group and making your members feel comfortable. When they feel comfortable with your presence, influencing them will no longer become that difficult.

Build a good reputation

You can't expect people to follow your lead if you have a bad reputation. You can be an influential leader if your followers see your credibility and honesty. Be honest when dealing with your team. Avoid lying to them or hiding some important facts. Once they find out that you are deceiving them, gaining back their trust will be extremely difficult. You will never become an influential leader if they don't believe you.

Provide positive feedback

Instead of focusing on the mistakes that your members commit, work on finding the good points on their performance, no matter how minor. Invest on means to encourage, motivate and reinforce your members, instead of imposing conditions and threats. By constantly providing positive feedback, your members can see your good side and your positive intentions, making it easier for them to trust you.

Admit your mistakes

A lot of leaders find it hard to admit their own faults. In most cases, they tend to put the blame on others, believing that their position makes them incapable of committing mistakes. Avoid being one of these kinds of leaders. Be a kind of leader who knows when he is wrong and admits it quickly. If you readily admit your mistakes, then you communicate to your members that you truly care about them. You are also showing them that you are fully aware about how your behavior and your mistakes can affect everyone in the group.

Be visible

Exceptional and effective leaders are those whom their members and followers can easily see, not just hear. Several leaders today fail to be visible to their members because of their extremely hectic schedules. Some of them leave their office without checking how their members are doing. Some leaders even hide in their office to avoid dealing with others.

It is time to change this habit. As a leader, you have to recognize that it is the effort of your group, which makes your organization successful. Be with them and let them see you from time to time. Sometimes, a friendly hello to your team is enough to boost their morale.

Act on things quickly

You can be an influential leader if you show your members how you act on things quickly. Don't be too slow to take action. Note that if you take a lot of time to make a tough decision, delay taking action or procrastinate, then you are sending a negative message to your members.

To be an influential leader, you need to move to action right away because your members are waiting for your decision. This can be very motivating for your members. This can also raise their confidence and trust in your ability.

There are many ways through which a leader can influence people. Mentioned above are some of the most effective ones. After following these simple steps, you will notice that more and more people are believing in you, and are becoming more willing to follow you.

Chapter 16: Don't Be Led – Breaking The Invisible Lead

Being aware of your current situation, and how many factors in your life have been the result of someone else's thinking, makes the perfect setting for a change. It is time to really think about the actions you are taking and the things you are doing daily which are not what you really want to be doing.

As mentioned in the previous chapter, it is time to fill those missing pieces of your jigsaw puzzle with decisiveness and discipline, and start to learn how to use these abilities. Firstly, you need to remove the existing actions you take daily which you have been guided to take.

Take your time to look at your life from all aspects and consider if you are doing the things you really want to be doing, and remember that you have only one life to live. It is good to be an active person, but it is OK to drop the things you are not enjoying. This frees up time to replace them with new things you want to do.

You will always be a unique character with your own interests, so to pursue anything that does not match who you are is a pointless waste of energy and should be abandoned. There is no room in the life you really want, or the life you wish to create to be following a path not suitable for yourself. This would be like an ambitious race car driver being a postman, a scientist being a retail assistant, an astronaut being a waiter/waitress, someone who enjoys sport but doesn't find time to exercise, someone who enjoys film and acting but instead goes to dancing classes because his or her friends do.

Imagine the mind as a wheel on a car, when the wheel is put on the car it is usually balanced with weights to make sure it rolls in a perfect line. If one wheel on a car is unbalanced (this can usually happen due to hitting a pothole), a vibration will be felt when the car reaches a high speed, and it will not drive smoothly. This is similar to allowing others to influence your decisions. Your life will not be smooth, and the journey will be uncomfortable. Therefore, you have to start to balance your own mind by removing the damage that has been caused by others. If you can correct your thinking, by removing all external forces, and focus solely on what you would like to do and where you would like to be going, you will find your life and journey much more satisfying, and it will roll a lot more smoothly.

Chapter 17: Communication And Management Skills

The billionaire that we quoted earlier, Richard Branson, believes that communication is the major tool that you need to be able to use when working with people. He says that without good communication, a company can fail. Good leadership demands it. If a leader rules by using intimidation, that makes them a dictator and that doesn't go down well with people who have been employed because of their skillsets. The good thing about communication is that it can be learned. People whose weakness is communication have been taught to communicate more effectively and have achieved great things. There are quotations in an article on Richard Branson by Forbes writer, Carmine Gallo, that a graduate got his dream job by practicing interview tactics for over 8 hours before going for the interview. In fact, the team were so impressed by the way that he communicated that they asked him to be a role model for other people within the company. When your communication skills are honed, you can win over those around you and get exactly what you want from them with very little effort.

The way that you give presentations can count as well, because when you are able to communicate effectively, you sell ideas. From the top of the career ladder, that's a very useful skill indeed. It helps you to sell your ideas and ideals to the employees who will fulfill those ideas and who can get inside your mindset so that what they come up with actually complies or excels that which you envisioned. We said in an earlier chapter about the importance of socializing. The reason for the importance is because you are likely to make contacts that further your career, but there's another very good reason. The more often you communicate with people, the easier it becomes. It becomes second nature to explain things to the public if you are accustomed to doing this, so the more you mix with people, the more your ideas propagate.

Your management skills are vital too. The kinds of skills you need to work on are your approach to employees. If an employee fails, you have to work out whether to cut your losses or whether it is your training program that has caused the failure. Often there are crossed wires and when you uncross them, you grow as a leader and your workforce grows under your leadership. If you blame everything upon others, it doesn't bide well in the management stakes because there are always reasons for under-achievement. If you learn what those reasons are by getting to know your workforce, then you grow and are able to face greater problems in the future.

Management skills include:

Knowing who to delegate to

Knowing your team strengths and weaknesses

Being able to provide employees with training

Keeping in touch with results

When you employ qualified staff that know what they are doing, the amount of direction you have to give that staff is less, but they still need to feel like they are part of something exciting. If you reckon up the amount of hours that people spend in the workplace, you need to be able to produce an atmosphere in which people are enthused. It all comes from the top and having team efforts really does help to enthuse members of staff. If you find that there are clashes of personality of that the atmosphere of the office is not sufficiently productive, you need to be able to tackle problems and make moves to improve the work environment so that your employees produce more work.

Richard Branson has a handy tip for leadership and it's one that leaders can really use to help them to improve the efficiency of the workplace. He says that when he employs people, he does so to fill his weak spots. Recognizing what someone can do better than you can helps you to be more effective and that's really good advice. The other thing that he does which I would say was sensible practice is to promote from within the company because you get to experience company loyalty from members of staff who work toward that promotion, rather than stagnating while strangers are employed in the top jobs.

There are leaders who put emphasis on keeping up with the competition, although Branson does not agree with this. He thinks that the management skill is to actually find voids in the market, or needs that the company can fill. If you do this, you don't need to worry about what the competition is doing. With people who are qualified in all areas of your business, brainstorming is therefore essential, as is listening to what the workforce is saying about what the public wants.

Being open to learning at all times is the most vital skill you can have. If you think that you are a leader because you know everything, then it's a sad reflection on your leadership skills. Leaders who are open to improvement learn more about what makes companies tick and are able to come up with innovative ideas that help them to excel in the market rather than stagnate.

Chapter 18: 7 Steps To Growing A Successful Team

The greatest leaders mobilize others by coalescing people around a shared vision.
—Ken Blanchard

1. Form a Single New Team: While adding new members to a team that has already experienced success can be tricky, it is possible. Spend some time ensuring the new group bonds and there are no instances of an us versus them mentality forming.

The team should be encouraged to participate in activities that pull people out of their day-to-day group interactions and force them to interact with the team as a whole. The time the group spends solidifying should be both planned and spontaneous as to form a true team mentality you need the team to be able to interact casually.

2. Focus on Performance: Do your best to ensure that interacting with the entirety of the team is the normal course of action. Do what you can to encourage teamwork with your actions and make thoughts of the new whole team commonplace.

Be sure to use your leadership skills and trade on your reputation for being a good listener to get a feel of how the new team is coming together. Don't make uniting the team feel like it is at the forefront of your thoughts, encourage it through day to day actions.

3. Encourage on Participation: When integrating new team members, it is easy for some members of the team to fade into the background while others take center stage. A good leader is aware of

this fact and ensures that everyone is equally involved when it comes to providing input, making decisions (where appropriate) and seeing those decisions through. In the early days after adding new team members it is important to shake up everyone's regular routines to avoid forming negative work habits.

4. Build Confidence: When adding to an existing team it is important to ensure the existing team members do not feel as though they are being replaced or that the team is expanding for negative reasons. Likewise, it is important to ensure the new team members do not feel disenfranchised in their new roles.

The best leaders are those who strive every day to encourage their team's commitment to one another as well as their confidence in the effectiveness of the team as a whole. Be sure to cultivate an atmosphere that encourages your team to take risks, that is the only way they will grow.

5. Facilitate Opportunity: When new team members are added it behooves the team leader to orchestrate opportunities for team members to put their best feet forward. When done in a subtle fashion it allows the team to find new people to fill traditional roles or for those who held the roles before to reassert their desire to continue.

6. Find a Common Goal: Nothing unites a new team faster than sharing a common goal that must be accomplished sooner rather than later. As the leader, you must provide the vision the team needs to find this goal and clearly articulate the ways in which this new team is the best team, in fact the only team, for the job. Your team members want to be successful they are simply relying on you to show them the

best way they can reach their full potential.

7. Notice Greatness: One important part of being a leader is finding others with leadership skills and nurturing them to carry on after you have gone on to bigger and better things.

By providing team members opportunities to lead themselves and set their own objectives you are helping to grown a future generation of leaders who will be able to more competently do their jobs because of the opportunities you provided them.

Having team members that you and the other team members can rely on to provide leadership functions in your absence will only make your new team fell more cohesive and be more productive.

Chapter 19: 10 Tips To Become A More Effective Leader

Being able to lead is important. However, there are those leaders, who are considered ineffective, thus they are not really giving any type of value as a leader. This is not a situation in which you want to find yourself. That is why it is in the best interest of every leader out there to learn how to become an effective leader. The following ten tips can be helpful in becoming an effective leader that people respect and will listen to.

Be the example

Leaders who led by example, instead of yelling or telling others how to do things are going to be more effective. The idea is that if you set the tone for how you expect others to act, they are going to follow your example.

Be humble

Though you may be the leader, the one in charge, be sure that you are giving credit where it is due. This is something that employees are going to highly respect, and it will make you an even better leader.

Your communication must be effective

You must have the ability to communicate ideas, directions and the like to others effectively. There should be no room for misinterpretation, as this can cause the project to run slower and will result in you looking incompetent.

Meetings should be productive

Having a long, drawn out meeting does not mean that you covered more information. In fact, the opposite may be true. To be a truly effective leader, have meetings that are short, but are full of helpful information.

Know what your limits are and stick to these

You should have limits defined from an early point in any working relationship. This is going to allow those who work underneath of you to know what is expected and what will not be tolerated. This will make the workday much easier for you, as there will be less confusion and issues.

Find someone with whom you can mentor from

Even the most effective leaders out there have modeled their behavior after one or more mentors that they have had. These mentors can be a great source of information when you run into issues.

Be aware that business also involves emotion

Though many are led to believe that emotions are absent in business, this is not always the case. You should realize that emotions will come into play and there are situations in which you can show that you do have a heart.

Be sure that you realize what leadership issues can arise

This is something that we will be talked about in a later chapter, but be aware that pitfalls are around every corner. If you expect these pitfalls, you will have a better chance of figuring out a solution and walking away from it without any real damage.

Mistakes are meant to help you become a better leader

There is no leader out there who has not made mistakes. However, these mistakes are meant to be a learning opportunity. Learn from these mistakes so that you do not make them again, thus effectively becoming a better leader.

10. Always look for improvement

No one is perfect, and this is especially true of leaders. You have to look at ways to improve your leadership, even when you feel that you may be the best leader out there. There is always room for improvement and an effective leader looks for methods constantly to implement into their leadership style.

Through implementing these tips into your leadership style, you will start to see improvement. Workers are going to have more respect for you, and you will find that it can make the workday run more smoothly.

Chapter 20: The Importance Of Leadership In Business

So the question remains: what exactly does leadership mean? Leadership is the process in which one person is chosen to help influence the attitude, behavior and thoughts of the people around them. People, who are leaders help to guide us in the right direction, help to inspire us to work harder and they help us to see what lies ahead of us. It is no secret that without leadership every human on the planet would quickly disintegrate into conflict and argument. This is because every human being sees the world differently and thus acts differently in their own actions, behaviors, feelings and our own different solutions.

Leadership helps to unite humans as a whole and help to point every single one of us in the same direction to work towards a common goal. However, a leader is not a leader without a certain amount of followers and these followers will not come immediately to stand behind a person right off the bat.

When it comes to identifying true leadership, it is often hard due to many instances of false leadership. All that false leadership is that it is a form of pretending and the person "leading" has no problem dropping their duty the moment they face trouble. However, there are many people in this world who wish to become leaders, but they aren't meant for that kind of destiny. These false leaders claim that they are leaders and they pretend they are setting a set course of direction and inspiring the people that follow them. More often than not however, are pretending.

There is an old saying that claims, "if you want to become a leader, find a parade and run to the front." This saying can be used to describe a false leader, because even though you run to the front of a parade, you are actually not leading it. Even in a parade a person is not really leading it unless they are choosing the direction it is going towards. A false leader may be at the front of a wave of people, but unless they are leading a direction to which the people are following, they are not leading them.

When it comes to leadership, many people do not realize that it can be used for both good and ill will. An example of this is Hitler himself as he was able to lead the German people that followed him but he led them in an evil direction. Hitler was a great leader, but he used his leadership skills for terrible uses and was responsible for murdering and torturing innocent people.

In the business world, leadership skills that are used for bad purposes are used to exploit others. In charitable organizations these people use their leadership skills to help benefit themselves rather than the people they claim they are trying to help. Either way there is different ways leadership skills can be used, but it is important to understand that they can be used to bring good things to people around the actual cause as well as evil things such as war and famine.

Why Is Leadership Important?

Leadership is important for a variety of different reasons. Regardless of where the leadership is needed whether it is at home or in a work environment leadership is important in every aspect of our everyday lives. Some of the reasons why it is important include:

1. Helps to provide a direction for both our families and our co-workers to follow when we face unstable times in our lives.

2. Help to set a positive example of what honesty is truly about and what it means to have it in everyday life.

3. Helps us to provide a safe and stable balance in our everyday lives between our work and family.

4. Leaders help to provide a stable and safe environment to help children to learn and grow up to be productive and intelligent adults.

5. Help the people in your life to start their own business, find whatever their passion may be or help the people around you to

lose weight in order to become the people they wish to become, as they grow older.

6. Help everyone around you to follow both their passions and their dreams. In today's world people need to realize that in order to seize the numerous and valuable opportunities around them, those who are destined to need to rise to lead others in order to achieve greatness for themselves. Though we may believe that only certain men and women who possess the qualities needed to lead people around them, ordinary people can become leaders as well, as long as they put their minds to it. Ordinary people are the ones who have the power to create great changes that the world needs, solve problems that others cannot solve and lead those that need their help. The only way ordinary people can do this however, is to believe in themselves and work to helping the people around them to work towards a better future.

The Seven Essential Principles of Leadership

In order to have effective leadership skills, there are seven essential principles that every leader must follow. As with anything else, leadership is not something that can just be done without thinking about it first. While leadership may come naturally for some people, for others who are thrust into a leadership position must practice and use these principles if they wish to succeed in leading others toward a brighter and more efficient future.

1. Must Be Patient

In order to become a great leader, a person must have great patience and must have excellent self-control when handling difficult situations. The act of leading others is not an act that can use a "soft" touch, as that will not help others to follow you towards the direction you want to lead them to. As a leader, even if you lead with love you must remember to hold the people around you accountable for their actions, but you must remember to do it with both respect and patience. Remember, when you lead others to follow you, you do not do it simply because of the performance you want; you do it to protect the dignity of the people who follow you.

If you are in a work setting, then your primary goal should be to train your employees to the best of your ability, whether it is in public or in private and it should be done with respect, patience and love. If you are leading your family at home then the same must be done as these people know you intimately and it could have catastrophic results if you lead them wrong.

2. Must Be Kind

In order to lead people, you must lead them with kindness and attempt to show encouragement and enthusiasm no matter what you are trying to accomplish. By leading with kindness you are creating and maintaining the right atmosphere in your environment whether you are at work or at home, so that your family or employees are able to deliver whatever it is you want them to deliver such as paperwork, behavior or customer service.

The best way I can describe this is to say for example a person you are leading is a bank account. Your primary goal is to make a deposit into their emotional "account" so that that account can grow into something you never would have imagined. When you show kindness to those around you, the goal is to give at least three praises to everyone admonishment. Using this ratio helps to ensure that you are showing the right amount of kindness to those around you. Kindness eventually leads to the people around you becoming loyal and enthusiastic to your cause and will help them to follow you willingly.

3. Must Be Trusting

Another thing that you need to do in order to become a great leader is to gain the trust of those you wish to lead and to place confidence in them that you are an ideal leader. Trust works in two ways. In order for a business or a home to run efficiently, a leader must trust the people around them and the same goes for the people looking to the person who is leading them.

In order to gain other people's trust and to give them the confidence needed to follow you the key is to listen well to each and every person and to do so with interrupting their thoughts with your own ideas. Another thing to keep in mind is to also let the people around you to make their own decisions in the acts they are primarily responsible for as this will help them to be confident in your own leadership skills.

By trusting the people around you and by them trusting your leadership skills helps to build a positive environment and will eventually lead to positive morale and trust in the long run.

4. Must Be Unselfish

Another thing to keep in mind in order to become a great leader is to be unselfish and to think less of you. You need to think of the people around you more often than yourself from time to time. The same goes for the organizations around you as well.

When it comes to leadership, it means that those of us who wish to lead are given the responsibility of giving up our time and our resources responsibly and properly. This responsibility often includes the responsibility of delegating which nearly every leader will need to participate in. Not only will delegating be rewarding and efficient for you, but it will also help you to become selfless and help others to view you as such. This helps to show others the respect you have towards them and make them much more willingly to follow you in the long run.

One way you can think of those around you other than yourself is to start and organization within your own organization in which you help the people around you who are in need. You can donate to these people and help countless people around you when they really need it.

5. Must Be Truthful

In order to become the best leader that you can be the key thing to do is to be as truthful as possible and make sure you know how to act in a corporate setting and in your own personal setting. This is often referred to as leading with love as you lead others by giving them truthful and loving feedback in order to make whatever they are doing better for not only the organization, but for themselves as well.

For many people who are not used to leading with love will feel that this is strange and foreign for them and greatly puts them out of their own comfort zone. However, it is perhaps one of the healthiest ways to lead and helps to give leaders an opportunity to grow their organization or home life to great lengths. When leading the people around you, leading with honesty and giving them truthful feedback about their performance regardless of what they will feel is a way to show the people that you care about them and want to lead them in the right direction.

6. Don't Forget To Forgive

When it comes to having excellent leadership skills, leaders must not forget to be forgiving and to forget about holding on to grudges, as this is something that has the potential to harm your leadership over others. While forgiving people is sometimes an agonizing process and hardly ever leads to a happy ending, it is something that needs to be done regardless. I am not at all telling you that you need to ignore whatever rules and policies you have set forth. What I am suggesting is that you try to soften your own heart just a little bit and be willing to forgive others regardless of the circumstance.

While it may not be the easiest thing to do in the world, forgiving people is the right thing to do in the long run.

7. Be Dedicated

One of the most important things you can do as a leader is to make sure that you stay dedicated to the task at hand and to make sure that you stick to your values regardless of the circumstances. If you are the type of leader who leads the people that follow you with love and others do not understand what it is you are doing, simply forget them and continue leading them your way. Leading the people that follow you in a dedicated fashion is very important regardless if you are given approval or not because others are most likely to follow you willingly than others that do not lead in your fashion. Remember, a wise leader is one that dedicates him or herself to the task at hand regardless of what other people think and choose to lead their people with love. Leading with dedication is one of the best ways to lead any organization and while it may not be easy, it is the right thing to do.

Chapter 21: Learn To Be Trustworthy

Your team should feel comfortable coming to you whenever they have questions and other concerns. You need to display integrity so that your team will respect and value your leadership, and to do that, you have to be honest and encourage your team to do the same.

If you don't know how to instill trust in your team, here are a few tips that might be of help:

Show that you are passionate about your work – If you demonstrate your passion about what you do, your team will reciprocate. They should see that you actually like working for the company and you care about it and the other employees' welfare. One of the best ways that you can show your passion is by wearing the merchandise that your company hands out, and you are also active in the company's social media activities.

Share what you know – Would you trust a leader who has little to no knowledge about the industry? If you want to become a trustworthy leader, you need to show your team that you have technical knowledge that extends beyond what they have, or at the very least you should know what you're talking about. Employees tend to respect leaders who actually worked their way up the corporate ladder rather than someone appointed to the position without any prior experience or knowledge.

Stay true to your words – It might be tempting for a leader such as yourself to promise grandiose things to your team to raise their morale, but you need to make sure that you can deliver on your promises when the time comes. It is almost impossible to regain the trust of your team when you fail even once to keep your promises.

Trust your team – If you want your team to trust you, you should trust them as well. You can show your team your trust by not second-guessing their decisions and opening yourself for any suggestions. Remember that your ultimate goal of becoming a good leader is to help your team to become the best that they could be; if your team is successful their achievements will reflect on you as well.

Chapter 22: Commitment

Commitment is what separates the doers from the dreamers. It refers to the dedication to a certain organization, belief, cause, or willingness for involvement. A leader who is committed to his company always shows up, follows through, and sticks with it. If there are more people committed to the organization, there is a greater momentum generated to get things done.

Commitment is actually the backbone of an organization or group. It is what gives your organization strength. The more committed you and your employees become, the more effective all of you become at influencing other people. When all of the people in your company act with commitment and determination, more people will give you their attention.

As a leader, you can show your commitment by not being discouraged easily. You must not give up, no matter how difficult the situation becomes. You also have to set an example to those who do not have the experience or confidence to go through difficult times. Take note that people tend to cooperate at higher levels when they share their commitment. It is commitment that fosters trust, care, and camaraderie, which are all necessary to keep an organization going.

Say, for example, one of your employees comes up to you and informs you that he is going to be late in submitting a project. If you are truly committed to this employee, especially since he has already done a lot for the company in the past years, you may feel disappointed. However, you will also take into consideration certain factors such as he may have other things to do or perhaps the project is too much to deal with. Instead of getting angry, you may offer this employee some help.

Then again, if you are only half-heartedly committed to this person, you will point fingers and blame him. You will also begin to think of the past mistakes or poor work that he has done in the past. You will forget all the hard work this employee has put into the company. As a result, you will feel negatively towards this person. You may even feel that this kind of situation is already "expected" of that employee.

If you are committed to your employees, you are loyal to them and you trust them. You do not mind going out of your way just to see the good in them as well as provide them with your own energy and time so that they may succeed. If your employees are also committed to you, they will do the same. They stay loyal to you and they become willing to make sacrifices to help you.

When the level of commitment goes down, people turn cynical. They begin to search for faults and flaws. They also stop exerting effort to help one another. You have to realize that as a leader, a commitment model is necessary for your leadership. You need to gain commitment from the members of your team.

Likewise, the members of your team should be committed to you in order to trust your decisions. They should also be willing to give you their energy and time to help you achieve the goals of the team. Team members who do not have faith in their leader tend to question every little request as well as hold back. When your team has strong levels of commitment, you are able to go above and beyond. This yields great results for your team.

Chapter 23: Body Language Is Key To Leadership

"People need realness, reality. People can sense when someone is being pretentious or fake. It's because you feel it; you see it in someone's body language."

AfroJack

SIGN UP FOR MORE FREE EBOOKS !

Human beings are social beings — this we have already established, which is why we have gone into such depth about how one needs to interact and how one needs to focus heavily on the aspect of effective communication. What they say, what they don't say, and even how they say it are things we haven't talked much about. It is one of the most important things when it comes to creating total self-confidence, and that thing is Body Language.

From the beginning of time, mankind has depended on the basics of body language to communicate the simplest of nuances, such as the touch of a lover or the tap of a friend. These multi-faceted silent gestures have been the subject of human interpretation, to such an extent that the human brain now associates certain forms of behavior with certain future actions. We are going to look into in that behavior and actions in this chapter. What does our body language say about us, and is it what we want it to say?

Let's start with the common forms of body language that is seen in people with low self-esteem. People with little self-confidence or with a small sense of self-worth tend to vary between being defensive or closed off. Both of these characteristics are identified by the tendency to cross one's arms or legs, a tendency to flinch or turn away when spoken to, or worse, a trend towards appearing aloof when being talked to.

Now, the upside is — YOU are no longer part of this group. So the likelihood is your body language has already changed a bit, but that doesn't mean it couldn't do with some additional work. Remember that even some micro face expressions can influence the interpretation that other people might have of you, at first sight, so you need to ensure that you don't have any negative micro-expressions at all. You are all about projecting a sense assurance now — so act like it! Take control of your body. Of course, this does not mean that you should try to control every muscle in your body as you communicate with others; that will make you come off as some strange, socially awkward person.

So instead, take a deep breath and calm down. You are going to do everything I just said you couldn't appear to be doing, but you are going to do so without any of the telltale signs.

How?

Well for starters, we are going to get rid of all the defensive posturing you are prone to. No more crossing your arms or legs, or twitching while you speak to someone. Instead, try to make sure you maintain eye contact and make subtle inward movements with your hands if you do move them. Inward hand movements tend to give off the idea that you are connecting your words with your actual self. It helps to project your confidence to the person you are speaking with, which is exactly what you want to do.

It may sound cliché, but smiling also helps change your body language. Think of the person you are having a conversation with as your client. It's your job to make them feel welcomed and comfortable. Smiling, or having positive interactions before you start an important conversation, can go a long way in helping you build better, more positively charged relationships.

Knowing how to properly use body language can be an imperative tool that can help you better interact and meet people along the way. Make sure to remember the most important traits of body language on a confident person:

• Walk as if you own the place - head and chest up, stomach sucked in and smiled.

• Maintain eye contact with whoever engage in conversation. It might be awkward at first but the more you do it. the more natural it becomes.

• Greet people on the street, even if you don't get a response back

• Use hand gestures when you talk if front of large groups or even on one on ones

Chapter 24: Be A Positive Influence To Others

The leader of the group is considered the highest authority and is the person who is expected to have expert knowledge on the subject matter. In this light, a leader is his followers' role model. To become a role model, he must exert positive influence to them. A leader who serves as a positive influence to his followers does not only help the group towards the attainment of their goals, but also helps his followers strive to improve themselves by emanating the positive characteristics of their leader.

How can a leader become a positive influence to others? Here are some tips:

• Practice what you preach: say what you mean, mean what you say – One way for a leader to establish credibility, authority, and legitimacy altogether is to show his followers that he means what he says and he says only the things that he means. His followers will respect him if they see that he is a person who is true to his word, one who does not change his mind often and one who does not impulsively decide on crucial matters. When a leader begins to promote this culture of practicing what he preaches, there is a great possibility for his members to adopt this positive attitude.

• Accommodate negative criticism – A leader has a big responsibility on his shoulders – not only must he handle a group of people, but he must also make sure that everyone is in good terms with one another and he must ensure that the group succeeds in their task. In this, a leader cannot avoid receiving negative criticism, either from his members or from people outside the group. When this happens, a leader must be very patient and he must work on his flaws instead of responding to the negative criticism people throw at him. Practicing this positive habit will create a norm of patience within the group. On the other hand, a leader with a bad temper will surely receive greater negative criticism and will also not gain respect from his followers.

- Stay neutral, objective, and do not play favorites – One way to be loved and to be favored by one's members is to be fair and to not play favorites. When the group members see that their leader provides rewards according to merit and gives sanctions based on the rules, he will gain the respect of his members and his decisions will not be deemed as unfair because they are by the rules and are not made based on the leader's personal preferences. It is difficult not to let one's emotions get in the way of making crucial decisions, especially when trying to get back at people who have committed a mistake against you. But as a leader, one must strive hard to be as impartial as possible.

- Be sensitive towards others – If there is a person in the team whose actions are the most monitored and the most evaluated, it is the leader. Every word he says and every action that he does are subject to public scrutiny. A leader who shows insensitivity will only gain disrespect and ire from his followers, but being sensitive to the group members' feelings and knowing whether his words and actions are offensive or not will create an atmosphere of respect within the group. Moreover, a leader who is sensitive to his followers' feelings is a leader who is loved. It will make the leader closer to the other members of the group, and when they share this bond of mutual respect, then most definitely his followers will not be shy to approach him when things go wrong or when they need help. Having members who are afraid of their own leader is detrimental to the success of the group – because being afraid of the leader will prevent members from bringing up problems to authority even if the members know that there is something wrong in their work. This will only result to the problem not being resolved immediately.

• Exhibit confidence – One way for a leader to appear authoritative yet respected is to exhibit confidence, both in himself, in his team as a whole, and in his followers as individual persons. In times of trouble, the leader's confidence serves as the anchor that keeps the boat afloat – it is the team's source of strength when they are faced with challenges. When things appear crucial, it is important that the leader shows his members that everything will be alright to avoid creating panic and to also boost his followers' confidence. Also, a leader who is confident that the group will succeed on their task is one who will work the hardest to produce good results.

• Be approachable – In trying to achieve a certain goal, it is important that the leader is communicative and is open to suggestions from his followers. When the other members of the group see that their leader is not approachable, they do not get to forward their concerns and suggestions even if they are of great worth and relevance. Doing so would miss the opportunity to improve the task further, because these unsaid ideas might be important.

- Focus on "we" and not "I" – A certain characteristic of a good leader is one who focuses on the "we" part of the task and never the "I", meaning that the leader recognizes that the task is a group effort and that he values the individuality of each and every member of the group and that he honors his members' ideas and not just his own. Focusing on the "we" makes a leader a person of cooperation and enables the members of the team to work harder because they know that they are important contributors to the team. Making the members of the group feel important is an essential part of being a leader, and if his followers see what it looks like to be a leader who recognizes the importance of group work and does not hog all the credit to himself, then it will create a sense of unity in the group and they will adopt the same attitude when they become leaders themselves.

- Demonstrate passion – A leader is expected to be the most hardworking and passionate among all members of the team, and when his members see that their leader is expressing enthusiasm and giving his full efforts into producing a good output, and then they will be inspired to exert their best efforts as well. After all, people will always choose to obey a leader who clearly demonstrates that he cares for the team's goals than to be led by someone who does not.

- Be humble – It is important for a leader to practice humility, because this is an important value that certainly inspires his followers. A leader who recognizes that success as a group effort and does not claim all the credit as his own is regarded highly by his followers. If the leader himself is humble and creates an atmosphere of humility within the group, then surely his team members would also observe the same practice.

- Be cooperative and collaborative – Even though the leader is the one giving the instructions and directing the progress of the group, his role does not stop there. One of the most important characteristics of a good leader, and one who is seen as a leader worth imitating, is one who works together with his members towards achieving their goals. A good leader must not only be collaborative, but he must also be cooperative – meaning that he observes the same rules as his members observe, and he does not make himself the cause of any delay.

- Acknowledge the group's successes – Together with exhibiting an attitude of humility, it is certain that a leader whom people look up to is one who acknowledges every success as something made possible by the whole group and not just himself or a certain number of members. Aside from being a positive influence towards the team members, this also strengthens teamwork.

- Observe proper work ethic – If a leader desires to inspire other people and to have other people refer to him as a good leader, it is important for him to observe proper work ethic; like obeying the rules, being strict with deadlines, being fair and honest, etc. One of the most effective ways for a leader to exert positive influence towards his members is to show them that he himself is observing proper work ethic, and this will give his members no reason not to.

- Be professional – Even though the leader is a friend to everyone, work is work and a certain level of professionalism must be observed at all times. Basic professionalism includes dressing appropriately, being on time, following the rules, and observing respect for every person's personal life. A leader who makes himself known as a professional is one who will surely be respected by his followers, and this respect will also serve as their reminder to observe the same level of professionalism towards their leader.

It is said that a person has successfully accomplished his task of being a leader if his followers wish to imitate his work ethic and if they are inspired to be just like him. It will take a lot of work, but keep in mind that other than succeeding as the leader who has helped the group achieve their goal, there is no greater achievement than gaining a sense of fulfillment out of causing a great and positive change in another person's life.

Chapter 25: The High-Yielding Dividend Stocks

One of the things that you need to know as a dividend stock investor is what a dividend yield is. Basically speaking, dividend yield is a ratio which indicates the amount of money a company pays out in dividends every year relative to its share price. This is usually in percentage form. The formula business people use to calculate the dividend yield is as shown:

Dividend yield= annual dividends per share/price per share

The yields for a current year can be estimated form the previous year's yields or by using the quarterly yield, then multiplying it by 4. The outcome is then divided by the current share price.

The dividend yield is basically used to measure the cash flow that you will be getting for the money that you have invested in the company. Without considering the capital gains, the dividend yield will give you the actual return on your investment. This is the percentage of your investment that you should be expecting to get at the end of every year.

The High-Yielding Dividend Stocks

Investors use the dividend yield in order to determine if the stocks of a certain company are really the right ones to invest in or not. An investor who requires a minimum stream of cash flow from his investment portfolio can get this kind of cash flow by targeting stocks that pay higher and more stable dividend yields. However, these high dividend yields sometimes comes at a cost of the stocks growth potential.

This is the reason all money the company is paying out as dividend is money that it is not investing back into the company. Those companies that pay a lower dividend yield reinvest part of theory returns back into the business and this is what comes with great capital gains for the investors. This means that the company is not making enough capital gains in the end. The only chance you have to gain more from the company is the gain for holding a stock. Once the value of your stocks go up, you can be sure that you will gain so much in returns but as long as you are receiving a high dividend yield, you can be sure that the other benefits go down.

So many things should come to your mind when you come across a company that is paying high dividends to its shareholders. The company might be undervalued at that moment and this is something to think about before you decide to invest into it. This could also be a plan for the company to attract investors. Companies that pay little dividends or no dividends at all are those that are overvalued or those that wants to grow their capital. There are companies though, which will pay a high dividend to shareholders, yet they are not undervalued. These are well established companies, and they are always the right choices when you are looking for somewhere to invest your money.

It is important for an investor to consider dividend yields of companies that they are investing in beforehand in order to determine the future dividends of those companies. You can use the recent annual dividend payment to determine this, or you can take the most recent quarterly payment, then you multiply it by 4 in order to approximate the current dividend yield of that company. Always know that the future dividend payments of companies are always uncertain, therefore you will never get a proper estimate. That is why stock investing is a highly risky affair that should be done with a lot of caution.

Safest way to invest in high-yielding dividend stocks

The investment world is quite tricky. The basic interests of investors are returns and safety and these interests are always in an inverse relationship. This means that you either go for returns and risk your safety or you go for the safety and forget about the returns. The problem is that investors are always looking to achieve both, which is possible but not really easy. Everyone is looking for a low-risk and high-yielding investment, which will give them benefits on both sides. Financial professionals would love to give investors just what they are in need of, and they are trying very hard to package investment products that will offer both safety and great returns. If therefore you are looking for high-yielding dividend stocks that are safe, you might be lucky. You however have to define and be clear about what you mean by safe and high yielding.

Safe is quite relative. Safe could mean an investment that will have zero downward risk, and you might not find anything to invest in when it comes to dividend stocks.

In as much as there are great benefits in investing in dividend stocks, the risk is inevitable. However, you can minimize the risk if you do not put all your money in just one company. Take advantage of mutual funds for instance especially those that are centered on companies with high-dividend yields. With these, you never lose entirely when the company is affected by market conditions.

Chapter 26: Work-Life Integration—Balance Is So Passé!

"I want to live while I am living—flexibility is important." –Erin

Just recently, Saturday Night Live featured a sketch poking fun at Millennials.27 It opened with a young woman frantically texting on her iPhone, approaching her boss and asking for a promotion.

The boss asks how long she's been with the company.

She replies, "Three days."

We get it. It remains extremely easy to poke fun at our Millennial friends. That being said, we still have much to learn from our Millennial colleagues. As a generation, they have come to understand some fundamental truths about the workplace that have taken us older generations fifteen and twenty years to come to grips with. The most productive leaders in today's corporate world do not look for work–life balance, but integration. Millennials have understood from the very beginning of their involvement in the modern workplace that work–life balance is a myth, and not just a myth, but a myth that they want no part of.

If we are honest with ourselves, we are all aware that work–life balance does not exist—in fact it's a boondoggle at best—and our Millennial colleagues have rejected that myth in its entirety. As soon as I was provided a Blackberry to assist me with fulfilling my job responsibilities, my work week changed from forty-five to sixty-five hours. I felt expected to be available and online, and while I take a good portion of the responsibility, technology actuated that expectation. The Millennial global view dispels the myth of work–life balance and demands more. If we as leaders are to motivate our Millennial colleagues in a way that provides them the opportunity to be as productive as possible, we need to recognize their desire and appetite for work–life integration.

Why then is the idea of work–life balance so contrary to a Millennial's point of view?

Millennial Passion

Millennials define themselves by their interests and their passions, and their work is part of that passion. They want to be engaged in work which they're passionate about, is meaningful to them and contributes in a real way to the benefit of society as a whole. Passion is an important factor in any individual success equation. When we love what we do, we are passionate about it and we give our all. It's when we're not engaged, and not passionate about the work we are asked to undertake, that our productivity goes down—along with the quality of our work.

We are all familiar with the oft quoted adage, "Do what you love and you'll never work a day." But is that true? Not likely, at least from my experience. I align myself with the thinking of Brad Warner, author of Hardcore Zen:

"…even the best job in the world is still just a job. Even Johnny Ramone said that being a rock and roll guitar player was a pretty good job, but that, in the end, it also sucked just like any other job."[28]

I have come to realize, unfortunately later in my career than I would have preferred, that I needed to figure out what work really and truly meant to me. Rather than searching for something to do that I loved, I needed to clarify what I wanted to get out of the work I was doing. Simply put, work is so much more than the day-to-day tasks we undertake, but rather, it feeds and energizes us to feel accomplished overall—Millennials get this, and right out of the box!

If we want to remain passionate about what we do, we need to remain connected to what interests us and engages our minds. Our Millennial team members reject the artificial imposition of the nine-to-five workday. They actually want to remain connected to those things that interest them, and if they're working on areas that are of interest to them, they will continue to want to be connected to those interests. If truth be told, the nine-to-five workday limits creativity, innovation and ideas.

Millennials see themselves as directly linked to their work, and if they are passionate about what they are doing, they don't want to disconnect. They want to leave the channels open to connect at whatever time is convenient, any and every time an innovation or exiting idea comes to mind. Moreover, Millennials admire and respond to leaders who display the same passion.29 They admire leaders who identify with the value of their work and are passionate about it as well.

During my interview process with a number of Millennial students, there was universal agreement that their productivity, and the perceived value of their work product, was directly linked to their passion. And if they were passionate about the work that they were given, they felt it was more than reasonable to invest much more than the standard forty-hour workweek to see that work delivered to the best of their abilities. Work–life integration, not balance!

My personal experience, as well as recent research, makes it clear that our Millennial tribe are not adverse to hard work.30 They are, however, unwilling to invest in work they see as not having value, or that they are not passionate about. That information in the hands of a leader wanting to empower the Millennial members of his or her team will allow some informed targeting of the work requested. The benefit will be engaged team members driven to produce quality product, because they are passionate about the work and see it has value to the organization!

Passion Drives Performance

A recent study undertaken by New York University in conjunction with comparative research tells us that 28% of the workforce are driven by purpose.31 By "purpose" we mean that intrinsic motivation that makes work deeply rewarding. Those people driven by purpose—and, to a great extent, our Millennial colleagues—see very clearly the linkage between who they are and the organization they work for. They not only understand that linkage but seek it out in aggressive fashion. They know what they want to do with their lives, and what they want to do with their lives they want to do with a sense of purpose.

Current research further confirms that those of us in the workforce driven by purpose outperform others in terms of position, money and influence.32 Do you want motivated Millennials? Engage them where their passions lie and give them a sense of purpose!

Passion Attracts People

It is paramount that we as leaders recognize that for Millennials, the very first interaction with the prospective employer influences their decisions in a powerful way. Studies have shown that the very first interaction makes all the difference in the decision to accept a job offer.33 Talent recruitment is a competitive arena. If in our current job market the vast majority of our potential hires are Millennials, then we need to ensure we hit the mark with that first impression. We need to ensure we articulate the vision of our company in a way which ignites passion and aligns itself with those criteria that drive those Millennial recruits.

In my interviews, there was an unmistakable weight given to the engagement factor when the students made a decision on where they would work. One of the students described to me an opportunity where he was offered a position at a very prestigious embassy, but which he turned down because he did not feel they wanted him very much. He felt like a number. He went on to take another position based on the interest demonstrated by the supervisors that interviewed him. Furthermore, those interviewed emphasized that they wanted their opinions taken seriously, and at the very least entertained, before final decisions were made. At the end of the day, people who know what they want and are passionate about its pursuit will not engage for long if those same values are not reciprocated.

The Passion Boat has Left the Station

The reality of the modern workplace has shifted, and the change is real. The modern workplace demands a different approach, and one that does not suggest that work–life balance is a reality. Aligning our approach to that of the majority of our workforce and teams sets the stage for high performance and achievement. So with technology making us available 24/7, the challenge for modern leaders is to find viable alternatives for integrating work and life, so that both can coexist.

Not too surprisingly, the answer is found in technology itself.

Our Millennials instinctively understand what we from other generations have yet to recognize. We are "anywhere" workers, and as such need to be supported through technology, to make that reality as seamless as possible. A recent survey led by the Unified Group indicated that the most successful teams were those where more than half of the team were located somewhere else.34 We understand that we currently live and work in a borderless world; a world where connectivity and technology make working remotely as productive as being physically located with the rest of our teams. No one generation understands that reality better than that of the Millennials.

If the most successful teams are those with nearly half their members located in other geographical areas, why not us? Our current teams may not need to be located in another country, but what about home, a coffee shop or the library?

Further insights stemming from student interviews were very enlightening. A large percentage of those interviewed wanted the option to deal with a personal issue outside of work at their own discretion, and then felt it completely reasonable for them to go straight home, connect remotely and finish what they had started, regardless of how long it might take. It does not sound at all like an unwillingness to work. Our Millennial cohort have quickly embraced the idea that productivity is not about location, but is about passion and drive. If that is the case, then we as leaders need to ensure that we provide the technology and connectivity to ensure that location is not an obstacle, but an option. In doing so we will once again contribute to harnessing the potential and the productivity inherent in our Millennial tribe.

One final thought on passion: in the past we valued a strong work ethic, and saw it as a characteristic to be envied and recruited. That definitely has not changed. However, in the past we defined work ethic very strictly. We saw it as staying in the office for fifty or sixty hours, always in the office, visible to all as an example. Optics outweighed efficiencies. Today's technology provides opportunity for the same commitment to happen remotely, and the time has come for us to move from overvaluing optics in favor of a modern productive workforce.

Chapter 27: Subtle Tricks To Influence People

As a leader, you want to become a master manipulator without the reputation of being one. When people think that you like to play mind games, they will be wary every time they are dealing with you.

Your influence towards others starts with how they see you as a person. You want people to like you. If they like you enough, they may give way to your requests and your suggestions.

You want your followers and your overseers to keep their guard down when dealing with you. You can do this by creating an impression of being dumber than you actually are. Most people are too vain to let others think that they are dumb.

Don't get caught when studying people

Effective leaders do not show signs that they are studying other people. When observing key followers, be subtle. If possible, only observe your key followers when they have no way of seeing you. You could do this behind one-way mirrors or through cameras.

When observing other people, your goal is to find out what motivates them. With most people, you learn this information simply by looking at their social media accounts. Most people will show the source of their passions through their personal posts. A parent for example, posts mostly about their children. This may mean that they are working hard because they want their children to have a good life. You may be able to motivate this type of follower by giving rewards related to their parenting needs.

On the other hand, a person who is always posting about shopping on his or her social media account may love luxurious things. He or she may be easily motivated with material rewards.

Use people's passions to motivate them

The best leaders adjust their methods of motivation based on the source of passion of the person they are motivating. Rewards for example, are the most common types of motivation used by leaders. However, rewards will only work for short-term goals. If you want to sustain your followers' motivated efforts, you want to align the goals of the company or organization to the goals of the goals of the person you are trying to motivate. If you are dealing with a family man for example, he may want to be promoted so that he can provide the future needs of his family. If you see evidence in your observation of that person that this is true, you mustuse this information to improve the person's performance in the team.

You can create a step-by-step plan to that person so that he will be promoted. In the plan, add tasks that you personally want him to accomplish. You could then tell that person that he would be considered for the promotion if he accomplishes the tasks in the action plan.

By doing the method above, you will be able to motivate the person to perform better. If you are considering more than one person for the promotion, you may let them know about it ahead of time. The person with the better skillset for the position should come out on top.

Avoid giving criticisms

Many managers try to boost other people's performance by pointing out the mistakes they made. Unfortunately, these managers were never informed that most people do not respond well to criticisms. Instead of doing well, people tend to perform less effectively when they are criticized.

When trying to influence others, you will motivate others better if you avoid criticizing their work. Instead of criticizing, suggest alternatives to what they are doing. For instance, you may point out that when you were in their position, you made many mistakes. You could then elaborate the mistakes that you do not want them to repeat. By stating it this way, you never criticize them for their mistakes. Instead, you are telling them that you did the same mistakes in the past and that you were able to improve your performance by doing certain changes.

Lower your followers' guard by being more relatable

Most people think that being a leader means that they should keep a perfect image. This is not always the case. If you are too perfect in the eyes of your followers, they may not follow your advice because you are not very relatable. People usually follow leaders that they see themselves in.

For instance, a group of students is more likely to follow a teacher closer to their age rather than someone significantly older. The younger teachers aremore likely to see the situation from the students' eyes. This shared perspective allows the younger teacher to bridge the gap between the older teacher and the students.

If you are not relatable to the eyes of the people you are supposed to lead, it will be hard for you to motivate them to do what you want. They will not trust you and they will always be on guard when they are dealing with you. When their guard is up, they are less likely to heed suggestions and advice.

To be more relatable to the people you are leading, you must show signs that you are just like them. There are many ways to achieve this. For instance, you could choose special occasions to bond with your followers. When bonding with them, participate in their activities to be accepted by the group.

You could also do this by spending time with the people you lead on regular workdays. For instance, spend your lunchtime with them or invite some of the more influential member of the group for dinner. You could win that person over so that he or she will introduce you to the group.

In more extreme cases, you could lower the guards of your followers by showing a sign of vulnerability. For instance, try standing up for the group against your own boss. By doing so, you will be able to gain the trust of your followers. While this is effective in winning over the trust of your followers, it is also risky. Effective leaders only do this when they are certain that their overseer will not get rid of them for doing so. If you trust your overseer, you can also stage the misunderstanding just to gain the trust of your followers.

Mirror the other person's actions

When talking with someone that you want to influence, use the mirroring technique to be liked by the other person. To use this technique, you first observe the little mannerisms of the person you are talking to. Some people for instance like to cross their legs in a certain way. Others have a compulsion to touch their hair when they are stressed.

You observe the little things that the person that you are talking to is doing. After few minutes, try to copy the gesture or mannerism. Also, make sure that the other person is looking at you when you do it.

When you mirror another person's gestures or actions, you are showing that you have similarities with that person. The person you are talking to will think of you as relatable and it increases the chance that they will follow what you are saying.

Influence people based on their need to believe

Humans are created with the urge to believe. This is the reason why most people still follow religions even though there is no proof that supernatural beings exist. People are mentally hardwired to have a sense of belief in something they are passionate with.

One example of a need to believe is our urge to find a good leader to follow. Certain types of personalities prefer to follow than lead. If you just create an image of an ideal leader, you will be able to win over these personality types. This is the reason why big companies often change their CEO in rough economic time. The new leadership creates hope in the hearts of the workforce. The newfound hope is more likely to motivate them to keep themselves motivated.

Your timing in taking the leadership position is crucial if you want to create this type of effect among the people you lead. Steve Jobs for example, returned to Apple when the Mac was struggling against other PC brands. His reentry to the leadership position created a hope among long-term Apple employees. This atmosphere also gave them the ability to hire new engineers for product development.

A good time to enter a leadership position is when the existing followers are discontented with the current leadership. If you enter the company or the organization at this time, even small achievements will be viewed by your followers as great wins for the group. This will motivate them even more to do better.

You may sustain the faith of your followers in you with timely wins for the organization. After winning a few small battles with your group, they will be confident enough to take on bigger challenges.

Remove factors with negative effects to the group's motivation

As a leader, it is your job to make sure that the working environment is conducive to working. However, every now and then, you will encounter factors that may affect the motivation of your followers in a negative way. It is common for example, for you to find members of the group who are negative thinkers. When negative thinkers voice out their thoughts, they usually affect lessen the motivation of the people around them. Sometimes, people who are going through a rough phase in their lives may also create a sense of negativity in the group.

To prevent these members from affecting the motivation of the group in a negative way, getting rid of them is a good option. If possible, you could also fire people who tend to lessen the motivation of the group. If this is not possible, at least, limit their interactions with the other members of the group that you are leading.

Chapter 28: Make Sure To Stimulate The Intellect

As a leader, it's important to ensure that it's not only you who learns and grows but that your subordinates also learn how to make the most out of themselves and out of the situation they're in. Intellectual Stimulation happens when leaders motivate their followers to be creative and innovative. As a leader, it's essential that you let your followers believe that they are destined to do great things and that if they work hard, use their brains, and are passionate with what they're doing, great results can happen.

How to foster creativity and stimulate intellect:

Here are some easy ways to make sure that your followers get to be creative and that no one remains stagnant. The worse that could happen is if there's no growth among your people and in the company itself.

Offer challenges. Create situations where your followers can assert themselves and can show you what they've got. This can happen by means of trainings, seminars, and team building sessions. This way, games could be played and you could have brain-storming sessions together.

Ask questions. Sometimes, the problem with some leaders is that they don't ask their followers questions. They think they know everything and thus, nothing happens. Even if you think you are smart enough already, remember that it's never wrong to ask questions and get the help of people. An effective leader is one who knows how to listen to the suggestions of others.

Developing an "I can do it" attitude. Remember what US President Obama once said? "If they say we can't do it, we say, yes we can." You have to let your people realize that whatever others may say, what's important is that they know they can achieve great things, especially if they work hard for it. Keep a positive attitude in the workplace and things will certainly look up for all of you.

Don't stick to norms. Don't be afraid to try new things out and don't be afraid to move past your limits. Think out of the box. If someone has a great idea and you think it could work for what your company stands for, go for it. If someone proposes an idea that you haven't tried before, go for it. It's always important to know how to ride the waves of change. This way, you can be sure that even if time passes by and no matter what happens, you will still be successful. You won't be able to make history if you only stick to the things you have already done. Don't be afraid to take risks.

Make the workplace a creative place to work in. Allow your followers to put whatever they want on their desks, provided that these things are not derogatory. Allow them to cover their desks with collages, or their favorite quotes or anything they want. A colorful, playful workspace is always better than a dull gray one. This way, they'll be more enthusiastic about working and they'll see you not just as a boss, but as a friend, too.

Observe. Learn how to observe what's going on in the world around you so you could get ideas as to what could be done and how you should be. Learn how to understand that change is inevitable and that the only way for people to relate to you and with what you're offering is if they know that it'll be useful for them and that you know what they want and need.

Don't overwork. Get out of the office after working hours, get an ample amount of rest and the next day, you'll realize that you're ready and actually excited to work again. Don't allow your followers or yourself to be overworked because the brain wouldn't work well this way. A creative mind is one that's able to get some rest, too.

Use Mood Boards. Mood Boards can either be corkboards where you can pin just about whatever that comes to mind—be it your vision for the future, pictures of places you want to go to or whatever it is you're feeling today. You can also use the website Pinterest, if that's easier for you. Bottom line is that if you can visualize something, it can happen because you'll work for it more and you'll be eager about it.

And, realize that it's important to learn something new each day. Never stop reading books, reading interesting articles and getting to know different types of people because this way, you'll get to learn more about the world you live in.

Keep these tips in mind and intellectual stimulation will certainly happen.

Chapter 29: How To Improve Your Management Skills

John D. Rockefeller: "Good management consists in showing average people how to do the work of superior people."

We often hear about management and leadership as being presented as two separate concepts. The truth is that these two are interconnected, more strongly than you might think or be aware of. A manager cannot hope to be successful without developing leadership skills, and the other way around. Management and leadership are not be perceived as separate concepts; given this powerful interrelation, it makes sense to work on developing management skills, first and foremost.

What are management skills?

Management skills actually refer to a number of actions you are going to take in your career path. For example, self-awareness is one of the most important management skills, making the difference between being an efficient manager and one who might have a negative impact on the company he/she is leading. Self-awareness can help one determine when a sensitive line should be overcome, in order to achieve the target objective set for the company.

The most important thing that you have to remember is that the development of management skills is actually a continuous process. If you want to be a good leader, you must always strive to improve such skills, especially since these will determine your success and the one of your organization. The development of management skills is not an easy process. On the contrary, given the complex knowledge and effort associated to the process, you need to stimulate yourself and not give up.

How to improve your management skills

Vision

Your vision is an essential element of success. After all, many successful companies have started with a dream. If you have a vision, it is important to share it with others and make sure they follow it. Communicate your vision to your employees and discuss about potential ways to achieve it. Allow them to ask questions and welcome their suggestions. If they are fighting for your vision, it will be infinitely easier to achieve it.

Up-close and personal

People will not listen to you, just because you are the manager. You need to get up-close and person. You need to be open and engage them in your vision. Take time to find out what motivates them, showing that you care about their own interests. The main idea is that you connect your vision to the possibilities they have to offer. How can you do that? Well, you can start by organizing informal meetings, get-togethers and even team building outings. All of these will allow you to connect with your employees and make them feel like they are a part of your vision.

Personal branding

Reputed managers know the power of personal branding and they are not afraid to use it. You have to work really hard to develop your personal brand, integrating your team in the process. Always think about the image you want to transmit to other people and the best ways to convey it. The personal brand of your company can be improved through simple measures: establishing a dress code for the personnel, choosing specific colors for your company elements and develop products/services in accordance to the said brand.

Power of gratitude

Gratitude can make the difference between satisfied employees and the ones who are already looking for a new job. If you want to be not a good, but an excellent manager, you need to show gratitude to your employees and team members. Accustom yourself to thanking or congratulating your team, especially when a difficult objective has been achieved. You might not be aware of it but gratitude is an excellent motivator and one that can do wonders, even more than financial remuneration.

Be fun

When you are first taught about management or leadership, the idea of fun is not part of the picture. We all know that managers/leaders should be stern, leading with an iron hand. But how accurate is this picture today? A quick look at some of the most successful companies out there, such as Facebook or Google, will demonstrate that fun is an essential element. You are the manager of the company and it is your job to make the work environment pleasant. Laugh, organize parties and encourage your employees to feel relaxed.

Start with your own self and integrate fun in more daily activities.

Acknowledge your own faults/mistakes

Perhaps this is one of the most difficult things for a manager to accept. But, if you educate yourself to acknowledge your own faults and/or mistakes, this will help you become a better manager. You will demonstrate to your employees that you are human as well, teaching them all about humility. When you work to accept your flaws as a human being, you will unavoidably gain the respect of the people who work for you. Admit to your mistakes and you will be one step closer towards achieving your objectives and the inherent success.

Read

It might sound like the obvious thing to do but reading can actually help you in becoming a better manager. Follow the example set by other successful people– for example, Warren Buffett, even at this venerable age, still spends two-three hours per day reading. He does that, so that he keeps up-to-date with the latest concepts regarding business, management and economy. Knowledge is power, even if we are living in an age where information seems to be changing by the second.

Constructive criticism

You need to be able to accept and provide constructive criticism at the same time, without being offended. A wise person once said that, if you are not open to constructive criticism, you are not open to growing as a person. Educate yourself to welcome any kind of criticism, as this will help you grow and develop, not only on the personal plan but also in connection to your company. Offering criticism is just as essential, as it will teach you to be open and honest. Such qualities might be perceived as aggressive at first, but, on the long-run, they will help you establish important relationships with other successful people.

Chapter 30: Management Principles To Follow When Dealing With Difficult People

As a leader, it is incumbent upon you to make sure that the workplace and the people who comprise it are not only productive and efficient, but also happy with what they are doing. For many, this comes as a tall order, mainly because there is no such thing as a utopia workplace.

Consider this: no two people are exactly alike. Each worker has a personality that is distinct from the rest. And while any manager would ideally prefer a united workforce, the fact of the matter is that there will always be a few individuals who will stand out for all the wrong reasons.

Difficult people exist everywhere. The nature of their character is one where the people around them are repulsed by their behavior. Worse, their character can affect the way others work and can even serve as a legitimate detriment in achieving the organization's goals.

In your case, it is your prerogative to get equally repulsed by them, but this does not mean that you will not be doing anything to remedy the situation. As a leader, you should hold yourself accountable in learning how to deal with these sorts of people and hopefully find a real solution to the problem at hand.

So how exactly do you deal with difficult people? Here are a number of essential principles you should keep in mind:

Develop a profound sense of self-awareness

If you find that some people you are directly dealing with are being difficult, it is better to take a moment to be introspective before launching an offensive. Take a good look at yourself and answer the following questions: Is it possible that you are the problem? Are you doing anything that makes other people around you react in a negative manner? Have you dealt with situations like this before? Do you see a recurring pattern in the way other people deal with you?

If you answered in the affirmative to any of the questions above, then now is as good a time as any to address your own personal issues.

Deal with the situation head on

If you are confronted with a situation where a difficult person is involved, address the situation right away. This is particularly important when the said difficult person is causing a directly observable impact on inter-office relations or causing a negative impact on the overall performance of the organization.

Remember that choosing to look the other way will not solve the problem. In fact, it may even aggravate it further. When employees, for example, feel that their leader is not doing enough to spare them from the toxicity brought about by a difficult coworker, they may develop a sense of resentment toward you.

Maintain objectivity and a sense of control

In dealing with a difficult person, it is necessary that you do not let your emotions or biases get the better of you. It is important that you maintain a sense of objectivity because otherwise you risk appearing to be favoring one party over the other. It's a careful balancing act. This also harks back to the previous point where issues with difficult people need to be nipped in the bud while you still can because the moment they morph into something bigger and destructive, it will be particularly hard to retain your control.

Direct confrontation is not really a good option, but it can be useful sometimes

One of the things that you should do away with is confronting difficult people in public. Doing so only serves to validate their behavior. In addition, you take the risk of provoking them into launching an emotional or physical attack, which is the last thing you would want to see in a situation like this.

That being said, there are circumstances where a public confrontation is a valid response. If constant communication and closed door discussion with the difficult person do not result in anything positive, then it's time to show a clear display of power and authority to put said difficult person in his/her right place.

Weigh things evenly, but always have the common good at the heart of your intervention

As much as possible, be honest with the parties involved. Facilitate an open exchange of ideas on how to best resolve the situation. Use humor if it's warranted. But know that in everything you do, your primary concern should always be geared toward the common good.

Your worth both as a manager and as a leader is measured not only by the title or position you hold. More importantly, a lot of it is based on your ability to deal with all kinds of people, including the difficult ones.

The next chapter discusses in detail how to assert your authority further through your creativity and imagination.

Chapter 31: Focus On Results

"Insanity: doing the same thing over and over again and expecting different results." – Albert Einstein

There's a saying that results speak for themselves. I agree. It's hard to justify your effectiveness as a sales manager for example if your group's sales are below target, even if you argue until the cows come home that you and your group did everything right by the book. But believe me, if your group's sales is 10 times the target, there will be no question about your effectiveness as a sales manager even if your compliance with company-taught practices is barely passing.

Being results oriented doesn't necessarily mean you'll be a slave driver to your group. No, may that never be. What I'm trying to drive at is you need to be able to set clear goals and objectives, the results of which can be objectively evaluated. Why? So that you can objectively determine if you and your group have successfully achieved your goals.

An example of a goal that's not so results focused is this: To make as many people happy as possible. Why is it not focused on results? First, it's not clear what it means for people to be happy. Happiness is a relative term, which is very hard to assess in a person. Second, the quantity "as many as possible" makes it practically impossible to achieve your goal. I mean, how do you actually know what's the maximum number of people your group can make happy? This becomes an unclear and moving target by which even a thousand "happy" people may not qualify as enough for success. You can't objectively determine if your group's successful or not.

An example of a results focused goal is this: To help at least 1,000 people move into their own homes within 12 months. Here, you have 2 clear criterions for determining whether or not your group is successful: if it's able to help a minimum of 1,000 people purchase and move into their very own homes and if it's able to do that within a year. It goes without saying that being able to move into one's own home will make them feel happy and that's a measurable indicator of how many people you can make happy.

Another benefit of being focused on results is easier evaluation or rating of your members, if you need to grade the people you're leading. It's hard to give a failing mark to a person using subjective reasons like "you performed poorly" or "you're not cut out for this sales position". By focusing on results, you don't have to justify your evaluations – the results will speak for themselves. You can justify giving them failing marks because they didn't meet the sales quota, for example.

The last benefit of being focused on results is you make it easier for the people you lead to know what it is exactly that they need to accomplish. Many followers get discouraged because they don't know how much is enough when it comes to following their leaders. For example, if you tell your subordinates or followers that they need to raise enough money to keep the group alive, how much is enough? They may think that $10,000 per member is already enough and after working hard to achieve it, they rest but only to be dismayed upon knowing that $10,000 per member won't cut it. Focusing on results makes things clear and achievable, which helps inspire and motivate people.

Chapter 32: Social Dynamics

Social dynamics in a working team should be friendly and supportive. Sometimes (well, quite often), they are not so, and a source of stress. You, as a team leader, should be particularly aware of such dynamics, and work in order to better them. If you want to do this, you should observe (discreetly) how your team members interact; you may notice, for example, and maybe through their body language, facial expressions, the tone of their voices etc., that there are conflictual (even if slightly conflictual) situations within your team. It may come to your attention, for example, that two people do not talk in a friendly way, but in a rather hostile way. Alternatively, you may notice some 'ice' between team members. If you overhear someone moaning about someone else, this, again, may be a sign of disaccord.

When you do this, do make sure that you do not poke your nose into their private matters; people who work together may (and often do) have their own private, personal stories. Your task is not to get the latest (or historical) gossip about who likes whom etc.; your task is to resolve problems.

Changing tasks, so that social dynamics change too (by shifting jobs around) may be a solution. Having social meetings where people can know each other in a different light can be a way forward too; the office drinks has become common practice in many countries, especially in the UK. Other social meetings have become popular as well, including, for example, the Christmas meal. However, if this is one of your chosen options, make sure that they do not become an obligation nor a burden. People should not feel obliged to come to the Friday drinks;

nor should attendance be related to promotion (a survey shows that people who attend such drinks are far more likely to advance in their careers than those who do not). You, as a team leader, should always be impartial. Finally, such meetings, especially meals and celebrations for festivities, may become formal affairs; this usually has some real problems; although leaders may feel that they offer a 'Cinderella night' to employees, the reality is that most people feel uncomfortable with formality (imagine being invited to a black tie night and not having the appropriate outfit, as has happened to the writer; you would end up having to pay a fortune for a night with your colleagues, while you may wish to spend such money on presents for your family). Thus, if you intend to have such socials, make sure that they are informal. In an informal situation, moreover, people are more at ease and are more themselves, thus they can really get to know, and hopefully like, each other better.

This chapter has been dedicated to improving social relationships within your team; however, it has focused on less conflictual problems. Unfortunately, sometimes, major conflicts break out on the workplace and you as a team leader will have to tackle them. This will be explored in the next chapter.

Chapter 33: Leadership Direction

Surging waves of the river if left undirected can create havoc, taking lives of millions and rendering million others homeless-a total catastrophe, but if properly nurtured and rightly directed these waves can render any pasture green, bringing life everywhere.

Every soul dreams but few are able to realize those dreams and are able to give shape to their ideas whereas the all-powerful time devours the rest.

These few who make history, who influences millions of other souls and who keeps on pursuing their dreams in spite of all adversities are considered to be the leaders.

A leader is one who leads by example; he always sees light when others see darkness and he never loses hope. He knows what he wants, why he wants and how to achieve his wants.

To know what we want and to also know how to achieve these wants is not the same thing. Many great ideas start with much fanfare but do not reach its final destination due to lack of proper direction.

If a leader wants to move in the right direction then he should know how to plan his actions and be well aware of all do's and don'ts while pursuing our cherished goal. If you fail to plan, you plan to fail, each one of us our aware of this fact still none of us know how to properly plan.

While planning to identify all the requirements which will be essential to accomplish the objective, study all the pros and cons associated with the objective, and outline the difficulties which he will come across in the future while pursuing the objective.

A brainstorming and division of work needs to be done along with the proper allocation of resources. Allocate the work as per the talent and liking of an individual. If an individual gets the work of his choice then he will definitely do the work with extra enthusiasm and energy.

A leader does not try to do all the things in one go rather he defines all the tasks and decide which things to do first and which to do later. Draw a time table for each objective and try to achieve the objective as per the schedule.

In case of coming across problems, first identify the problem and then try to understand the causes which led to the problem. After completing a particular objective, check the performance to find out whether the requisite standard has been achieved or not.

In case the work being not up to the standard, suitable changes can be done. Now finally a leader just needs to act as per the plan. He always tries to build a team and allocate the work as per the member's talent and liking.

A leader should be able to properly lead his team by always giving the members the right direction, by always motivating them and by communicating properly with them.

Leadership and communication

Great ideas are lost, great missions fail and empires disintegrate when people are not able to properly communicate with each other. Communication is the most important tool, in fact, the only tool, which helps a leader to lead his followers towards the coveted goal.

Communication is the process by which a communicator is able to communicate the message to the audience and the audience is able to completely assimilate the original context.

In communication, there is a sender (the one who is delivering the message) and the receiver (to whom the message has been delivered). The message passes through an external environment.

Technically speaking, there are three processes to a communication viz. thought, encoding and decoding. First a thought or an idea generates in the mind, these thoughts and ideas are then encoded in verbal or textual form and these thoughts and ideas are finally decoded by the receiver.

If different receiver decodes the message differently, then the original texture takes a beating and everything looks hazy.

The message needs to be communicated in such a way that the receiver should be able to properly comprehend the actual meaning of the message.

Communication can be verbal or written. During verbal communication, apart from the words the audience also takes note of the communicator's tone of voice, his body language, his hand gestures and his overall attitude-these all constitutes non-verbal communication.

Having proper eye-contact with the audience gives an impression that the speaker is giving lots of importance to the audience. Use of simple words, words which penetrates deep into the heart of the audience, creates a lasting impression in the receivers' mind.

Proper variation in the tone of the voice as per the context of the message is very much desired; do not be too fast or too slow while speaking. Too fast a communication makes the audience misunderstand you, while if you are too slow then the audience will soon get bored and you will lose their attention.

While speaking, be warm, friendly and approachable; always carry an eye-catching smile on your face, speak lively, always use comfortable words, try to grab the attention of the audience by using some interesting quotes or phrases but never deviate from the original topic.

Communication is a two-way process; hence, feedback is an important ingredient of effective communication. The communicator should be earnest enough to know what actually the receiver feels about his message; and with all sincerity accept the verdict.

You might think you have used the best sentences, the best words, the best phrases but if the receiver fails to understand your 'best' then it's best to through your 'best' into the best dustbin.

There are certain barriers to communication which need to be taken into account; as its proper understanding may help the speaker to understand the audience in a much better way before he actually starts communicating.

Understanding the culture of the audience is of great importance, some gestures or some words may be unacceptable in certain culture.

 Many times, the audiences carry some pre-conceived idea about something which needs to be dealt with very carefully. It is only through proper communication that a leader is able to effectively lead.

Chapter 34: Know How To Harness The Benefits Of Connections

If you want to be successful, you have to get along well with other people. The more connections you have, the more prospective customers or clients you could have. The more customers or clients you get, the more money you could make. You can even benefit from their free endorsements each time they recommend your products and/or services to other people.

Networking is a huge part of success. Some people have this notion that a lone entrepreneur can easily turn his dream into a reality. Unfortunately, that rarely happens. If you want to succeed as quickly as possible, you have to have great connections.

Think of Mark Zuckerberg. Many people believe that he is a lone entrepreneur. He was a technology disrupter and a college dropout, after all. However, he also had a lot of mentors along the way. In fact, Steve Jobs was one of his mentors. Zuckerberg actually credits Jobs for teaching him about keeping the company focused and forming strong teams. Because of his connection with Jobs, Zuckerberg was able to make Facebook a huge success.

Keep in mind that the more influencers you have, the greater your chances of achieving success. The most successful people use their networks strategically so that it would benefit them. As Keith Ferrazzi, CEO of Ferrazzi Greenlight and author of Who's Got Your Back and Never Eat Alone: And Other Secrets to Success, One Relationship at a Time, said, you should never quit keeping track of your "dream connections" if you want to be successful.

You are lucky because creating networks is much easier today. In the past, the Internet was not even existent, which means that there were no social media platforms, networking conferences, and e-mails. You have all these great things now, so make sure to use them to your advantage.

In order for you to be well-connected, you need to make substantive conversations. Do not just say 'hi' or 'hello'. Reach out to other people for a meaningful and substantial conversation. Speak about things that are valuable to both of you. You can use any medium of conversation, including social media, e-mail, fax, or phone call.

You also have to be brave enough to know the right people better. John Sculley, former CEO of Apple, used to sit around cafeterias to make himself approachable to the staff. If you are like most people who are too nervous or too tense to approach people like him, you will miss out on great opportunities. Don't be afraid to form a relationship because that might just be your ticket to a great job opportunity.

See to it that you add value too. Say, you wanted to book a popular celebrity to perform at one of your company's events. If that particular celebrity knows of your connections with another influential person and he is interested, it would be easier for you to book him. You can even develop a good friendship or partnership; thereby, adding more value to your connections.

You should also attend events in your industry. It does not matter how old you are or how high your position in the company is. You should always consider events as an opportunity to meet new people and create connections. You should also use them as an opportunity to maintain the connections that you already have with your peers, clients, and colleagues.

Furthermore, make sure that you take engagements seriously. It is not a good idea to take your connections lightly. Use the available technology to stay in touch with your connections so that you do not lose them. Every single one of your connections is important and can prove to be helpful in the future.

Chapter 35: Delegate And Get Things Done

Busy people must learn how to delegate if they intend to get things done. Often, there are not enough hours in the day to allow one person to do everything. Productive people come to know that delegating is necessary if one is to move forward. Productive people also know what can and should be delegated and how to accomplish that effectively.

What is outsourcing but delegating to skilled professional tasks that we cannot complete, from website design to public relations, cleaning our home to preparing the food for a cocktail party? The judicious use of delegating can be good for business profitability and healthy for organizational development. Employees can expand their competencies and learn how to add more value when workloads are occasionally shared.

When time and energy are scarce, or when we do not possess the required expertise, it makes sense from both a time management and quality control standpoint to delegate a given project and remove it from our plate, to focus on items that only we can do. If we hoard all the important responsibilities, it can lead to real or perceived controlling behavior, and that is counter-productive. How to delegate successfully is an important skill, and it begins with setting priorities.

Delegate responsibilities and not just tasks. Rather than merely assigning work to someone, which limits the sense of ownership, promote buy-in for the project at hand and loyalty to you and delegate the responsibility for leading an element of the assignment. Allow that person to shine and display creativity, analytical ability, systems and operations talents, troubleshooting prowess and whatever else it takes to manage that portion of the project successfully. You keep an eye on the big picture and do what is necessary to give that person the required resources and authority to do his/her part.

Accept that your way is not the only way. This could lead to some pleasant surprises and a better outcome than you envisioned. Everyone has a unique way of viewing and tackling a responsibility, and you are advised to respect those different perspectives and approaches and trust the person to whom you've delegated. Often, there is more than one road to the right solution. Focus on achieving the desired results within the desired time frame. Never micromanage.

Give clear instructions and sufficient information. Explain the big picture of the project and how the delegated element fits in. Provide project specifications for what will be delegated and confirm that the person understands. Make sure that the person has the authority to do what is necessary, along with the budget, whatever staffing, or other resources. Be clear about milestones and the project due date. Be available for help, if necessary.

Teach yourself to recognize when to delegate a project or elements thereof by first setting goals and objectives for your business, backed by strategies and action plans that will ensure their realization. Be candid about your strengths, weaknesses, and the timeline. Outsource/ delegate those responsibilities that you cannot do and focus on the result. Build a solid team that is ready to help you achieve your goals.

www.ingramcontent.com/pod-product-compliance
Lightning Source LLC
LaVergne TN
LVHW011933070526
838202LV00054B/4620